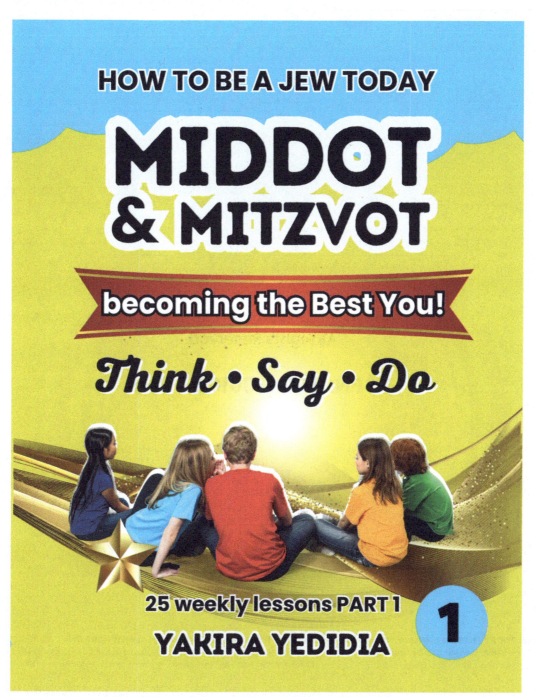

**CHAPTERS 1-12**

Copyright © 2024 by Yakira Yedidia
All Rights Reserved.

**ISBN: 978-1-961025-21-9**

---

**HOW TO BE A JEW TODAY- Middot & Mitzvot: Becoming The Best You. Think Say Do. 25 Weekly Lessons PART ONE**
Copyright © ℗ 2024 HEBREW GURU LLC. by Yakira Yedidia. All Rights Reserved. This book is protected by copyright. Reproduction of any kind, whether electronic or mechanical, is strictly prohibited without prior written permission from the publisher Hebrew Guru LLC. However, brief quotes may be used in book reviews.

The reader assumes all responsibility for any actions taken as a result of the information contained in this book.
Please note that the information in this book is intended to be for educational, general information purposes only and is not intended to be professional advice. While every effort has been made to ensure the accuracy and completeness of the content, the author gives no guarantees or warranties. For medical advice, readers should consult with a healthcare professional. The author is not responsible for any actions taken by the reader, including any losses, directly or indirectly incurred as a result of the content in this book.
Images used in this book are sourced from Canva Pro and have been customized for this publication.

HEBREW GURU LLC
Los Angeles, CA.
Printed in the USA
2024

To my family. My everything.

# This Book Belongs to:

# Welcome

## PART ONE

**"Middot and Mitzvot: Becoming the Best You - Think-Say-Do"!**

Get ready to embark on an adventure where **YOU** are the hero of your story.

Now we're not just talking about becoming the best version of yourself; we're going to live it!

Imagine learning from ancient heroes who didn't need capes to be legendary. You're about to discover their wisdom and use it to shape your own extraordinary story.

**But guess what?** This isn't just a bunch of words; it's your personal guide to real-life action!

**Here's a sneak peek:** in each chapter you'll find hands-on activities, superhero missions, and even your own to-do list for becoming the superhero of your life.

**And you know what's super cool?** You don't need any special skills to enjoy this adventure!

So, gear up, grab your imagination capes, and let's dive into *"Middot and Mitzvot"* – because being the best **YOU** has never been this much fun!

# CONTENTS

## BOOK ONE: CHAPTERS 1-12

**Intro Middot & Mitzvot** .................... PAGE 10

1. **Hachnasat Orchim** (Hospitality) .................... PAGE 21 — הַכְנָסַת אוֹרְחִים

2. **Shalom** (Peace) .................... PAGE 33 — שָׁלוֹם
   **Rodef Shalom** (Pursuing Peace) — רוֹדֵף שָׁלוֹם

3. **Din / Rachamim** (Justice / Mercy) .................... PAGE 43 — דִין/רחמים

4. **Teshuvah** (Repentance) .................... PAGE 53 — תְּשׁוּבָה

5. **Emunah** (Faith) .................... PAGE 63 — אֱמוּנָה

6. **Chaverut** (Friendship) .................... PAGE 73 — חֲבֵרוּת

7. **Tikkun Olam** (Repairing the world) .................... PAGE 83 — תִּקּוּן עוֹלָם

8. **Pikuach Nefesh** (Saving a life) .................... PAGE 93 — פִּקּוּחַ נֶפֶשׁ

9. **Shmirat Halashon** .................... PAGE 103 — שְׁמִירַת הַלָּשׁוֹן
   (Being careful about how we speak)

10. **Tzedakah** (Charity) .................... PAGE 113 — צְדָקָה

11. **Hodayah** (Gratitude) .................... PAGE 123 — הוֹדָיָה

12. **N'divut** (Generosity) .................... PAGE 133 — נְדִיבוּת

**Key Words** .................... PAGE 146

**Multiple Choice Quiz Answer Key** .................... PAGE 151

# IN BOOK TWO YOU'LL FIND: CHAPTERS 13-25

13. **Someich Noflim/Rofei Cholim** — PAGE 143 — סוֹמֵךְ נוֹפְלִים/רוֹפֵא חוֹלִים
(Lifting up the fallen/Healing the sick)

14. **Gevurah** (Heroism) — PAGE 153 — גְּבוּרָה

15. **Ometz Lev** (Courage) — PAGE 163 — אֹמֶץ לֵב

16. **Tochachah** — PAGE 173 — תּוֹכֵחָה
(rebuke, speaking truth to power)

17. **Bal Tashchit/Sh'mirat HaTeva** — PAGE 183 — בַּל תַּשְׁחִית/שְׁמִירַת הַטֶּבַע
(Taking care of the environment)

18. **Talmud Torah** (Studying Jewish text) — PAGE 193 — תַּלְמוּד תּוֹרָה

19. **Gemilut Hasadim** — PAGE 203 — גְּמִילוּת חֲסָדִים
(Acts of lovingkindness)

20. **Mechuyavut** (Responsibility) — PAGE 213 — אַחְרָיוּת

21. **Simchah** (Joy) — PAGE 223 — שִׂמְחָה

22. **Yosher/Emet** (Integrity/Truth) — PAGE 233 — יֹשֶׁר/אֱמֶת

23. **Yozmah** (Initiative) — PAGE 243 — יוֹזְמָה

24. **Manhigut** (Leadership) — PAGE 253 — מַנְהִיגוּת

25. **Ahavat Yisrael** (Love of Israel) — PAGE 263 — אהבת יִשְׂרָאֵל

**Key Words** — PAGE 281

**Multiple Choice Quiz Answer Key** — PAGE 285

# How are You feeling today?

Date: _____

# My Mitzvot & Middot Weekly Journal

Describe your mood at this moment with a word/emoji. Circle the word that fits best.

| _____ | Happy | Loving | Curious | Grateful | Surprised | Sad | Inspired | Nervous | Bored |

## Mitzvot Tracker

**Which mitzvot did you perform this week? Check off the Mitzvot and/or write your own.**

- ☐ Donated to charity.
- ☐ Helped a neighbor.
- ☐ Prayed at the synagogue.
- ☐ Volunteered at a community event.
- ☐ Respected others.
- ☐ Visited someone who is sick.
- ☐ Followed Shabbat rituals.
- ☐ Shared food with someone in need.
- ☐ Fed and played with my pet
- ☐ Studied Jewish text.

## Middot Tracker

**Reflect on your interactions with others**

**Check off the Middot you've practiced this week**

- ☐ **Kindness:** Helped a friend.
- ☐ **Honesty:** Admitted a mistake.
- ☐ **Patience:** Waited for a turn without getting upset.
- ☐ **Respect:** Listened attentively to others.
- ☐ **Compassion:** Comforted a friend in need.
- ☐ **Responsibility:** Completed chores without being asked.
- ☐ **Gratitude:** Thanked someone for their help.
- ☐ **Humility:** Accepted constructive criticism gracefully.
- ☐ **Courage:** Spoke up against unfairness.
- ☐ **Forgiveness:** Pardoned someone for a mistake.

**Write down your own if it's not listed**

Middot and Mitzvot – Becoming the Best You

# POSITIVE

# Do Jews Need to learn Hebrew?

Nope, being Jewish doesn't mean you have to be a Hebrew whiz. But guess what? Learning Hebrew is like discovering a treasure chest of cool stuff!

**What are the benefits?**

Learning Hebrew lets you connect with traditions, join in services, make friendships stronger, dive into awesome stories, feel a deeper connection to your beliefs, and even read from, and understand the Torah better. It's like adding extra sparkle to your Jewish journey!

**Wondering if you have to read Hebrew in this book?**

Nope! In "*Middot and Mitzvot*," we'll explore 25 important Hebrew terms related to Jewish values and ethics. Reading Hebrew is totally up to you, but if you want to give it a try, take a look at the Hebrew Guru Color Coded Vowels Method on p. 15 It's your secret weapon to read these 25 Hebrew terms like a pro!

And you know what's cool? Hebrew is easy to read because the way it's written matches how it sounds. The words on paper sound like the words when spoken, making it predictable and easy to understand. Let's make this journey awesome together!

# Hebrew Introduction

OPTIONAL

## The Hebrew Letters

| צ ץ | פ ף | פ | ח כ ך | ק | ו י | ג ז | נ ן | ד ר | ס שׂ | ה ל | מ ם | א ע | ב | ת | שׁ ב |
|---|---|---|---|---|---|---|---|---|---|---|---|---|---|---|---|
| TS | F | P | CH | K | V Y | Z G | N | R D | S | L H | M | A (SILENT) | V | T | B SH |

### The Hebrew Vowels

**The Hebrew Guru- Color Coded Vowels Method (CCVM)** is a tool that can help you read and pronounce Hebrew words correctly (Hence the Hebrew Guru logo)

**Hebrew has 5 vowel sounds;**
**A, E, EE, O, OO**

A as in AQUA,
E as in RED,
E as in GREEN
O as in ORANGE,
OO as in BLUE

A as in     E as in     EE as in     O as in     OO as in

fAther    fEd    fEEt    fOr    fOOd
bAy (as buy)   bEy (bay)   bEE   bOld   bOO
dAy (as dye)   dEy (day)   dEEr   dOr (door)   dOO (do)

In Hebrew, the vowel sounds are not represented by separate letters, as they are in English. Instead, Hebrew represents vowel sounds using small symbols above or below the letters. These symbols are called "nikkud", and they indicate how the vowel should be pronounced. (THE ✕ REPRESENTS A HEBREW LETTER)

| Aqua ✕✕✕ | RED ✕✕✕✕ | GREEN ✕י✕ | ORANGE ✕וֹ✕✕ | BLUE ✕וּ✕ | SILENT ✕ |

---

**Hebrew is read from RIGHT to LEFT**    אוּ  אוֹ  אִ  אֶ  אַ ←

SHA-LOM    (hi, peace, bye)    שָׁלוֹם

KA-FEH    (coffee)    קָפֶה

SHO-KO-LAD    (chocolate)    שׁוֹקוֹלָד

# Middot & Mitzvot

# What are Middot?

Welcome to the fascinating world of **Middot** and **Mitzvot**. Buckle up because we're about to discover the secret sauce to being:

## The best version of ourselves!

Imagine *Middot* as your personal superpowers, the qualities that turn you into a superhero of goodness. These are the traits that make us not just good people but amazing friends too.

Picture them like the coolest gadgets in your superhero utility belt - always there when you need them.

### 1. Kindness:
Remember that time you shared your toys with a friend? That's the power of kindness, our first *Middah*! It's like spreading joy and making others feel warm and fuzzy inside. So, whether it's sharing your snack or giving a high-five, kindness is your superhero sidekick.

### 2. Honesty:
Here comes another mighty *Middah* – honesty! Picture it as your truth shield. It's about telling the truth, even when it feels like doing a tricky balancing act. Just like superheroes always stay true to themselves, honesty helps you navigate through the ups and downs of life.

### 3. Patience:
Now, let's talk about patience, the Jedi-like skill of waiting your turn without turning into the Hulk. Ever waited for your turn on the swing? That's patience at work! It's a *Middah* that helps us stay calm and collected when things don't go as fast as we'd like.

# What are Mitzvot?

Next up, we have *Mitzvot* – the awesome rules that guide us on this incredible adventure called life. Think of them as the rules of the game, ensuring everyone plays fair and square.

**1. <u>Going to the Synagogue:</u>**
Imagine going to a magical place filled with stories, songs, and a sense of togetherness – that's the synagogue! Going there is a *Mitzvah*.
It's like joining a team and learning about our fantastic Jewish traditions.

**2. <u>Helping Others:</u>**
Now, let's unleash the superhero within you through the *Mitzvah* of helping others. Giving to charity, also known as *Tzedakah*, is like using your superpowers to make the world a better place. You become a real-life hero by spreading kindness and making a positive impact on others' lives.

**3. <u>Keeping Shabbat:</u>**
We also have the fun *Mitzvah* of keeping Shabbat – a day of rest and quality time with family and friends. It's like pressing the pause button on a busy week to recharge your superhero powers and enjoy the company of those you care about.

**In a nutshell:**

BEING    DOING

| Middot | Mitzvot |
|---|---|
| *Middot* is about BEING a good friend—share toys (Kindness), tell the truth (Honesty), and wait patiently (Patience). | *Mitzvot* guide you to heroic deeds–going to the synagogue, helping through *Tzedakah*, and observing Shabbat. These actions make you the hero your Jewish community needs. |

As we explore each *Middah* and *Mitzvah*, remember, you're not just learning rules; you're unlocking the potential to be the hero of your own story. Get ready for an exciting journey where you discover how being kind, honest, patient, and following essential rules can turn you into the coolest superhero in your community. Let's dive in, superheroes-in-training!

# Middot & Mitzvot fun quiz!

**Here are five questions with multiple-choice answers:**

**Question 1: What is a *Middah*?**

A. A superhero's secret weapon
B. A delicious Jewish dish
C. A special quality that makes us good people and friends
D. A type of Jewish dance

**Question 2: How would you use the *Middah* of Patience?**

A. To win a race
B. To wait your turn without getting upset
C. To jump higher on a trampoline
D. To eat your ice cream slowly

**Question 3: Which of the following is a *Mitzvah* related to helping others?**

A. Eating a big bag of popcorn
B. Playing video games all day
C. Giving to charity (*Tzedakah*)
D. Staying up all night

**Question 4: What does the Mitzvah "Keeping Shabbat" involve?**

A. Keeping a secret
B. Taking a day off from school
C. Taking a day of rest and spending time with family and friends
D. Eating only chocolate for a day

**Question 5: Why is Honesty a *Middah*?**

A. Because it helps us win arguments
B. Because it's a special quality that makes us good friends
C. Because it's a magic spell
D. Because it's a secret handshake

(Answers on p. 151)

# Chapter One

Hachnasat Orchim (Hospitality)

# HOSPITALITY

# הַכְנָסַת אוֹרְחִים ①

## Hachnasat Orchim

Did you know there's a special superhero value called *Hachnasat Orchim*?

*Hachnasat Orchim* might sound like a mouthful, but it's a fantastic Jewish value all about being an extraordinary host or hostess!

*Hachnasat Orchim* means welcoming guest, and it's all about treating guests with kindness.

The golden rule is treating others how you'd like to be treated, turning every gathering into a special, welcoming celebration!

How cool is that?

# How are You feeling today?

Date: _____

# My Mitzvot & Middot Weekly Journal

Describe your mood at this moment with a word/emoji. Circle the word that fits best.

| _____ | Happy | Loving | Curious | Grateful | Surprised | Sad | Inspired | Nervous | Bored |

## Mitzvot Tracker

Which mitzvot did you perform this week? Check off the Mitzvot and/or write your own.

- ☐ Donated to charity.
- ☐ Helped a neighbor.
- ☐ Prayed at the synagogue.
- ☐ Volunteered at a community event.
- ☐ Respected others.
- ☐ Visited someone who is sick.
- ☐ Followed Shabbat rituals.
- ☐ Shared food with someone in need.
- ☐ Fed and played with my pet
- ☐ Studied Jewish text.

## Middot Tracker

Reflect on your interactions with others

**Check off the Middot you've practiced this week**

- ☐ **Kindness:** Helped a friend.
- ☐ **Honesty:** Admitted a mistake.
- ☐ **Patience:** Waited for a turn without getting upset.
- ☐ **Respect:** Listened attentively to others.
- ☐ **Compassion:** Comforted a friend in need.
- ☐ **Responsibility:** Completed chores without being asked.
- ☐ **Gratitude:** Thanked someone for their help.
- ☐ **Humility:** Accepted constructive criticism gracefully.
- ☐ **Courage:** Spoke up against unfairness.
- ☐ **Forgiveness:** Pardoned someone for a mistake.

Write down your own if it's not listed

# HOSPITALITY

## More on Hachnasat Orchim

- **Friendly Faces:** Imagine you're having a big party, and you want everyone to feel welcome. That's where *Hachnasat Orchim* comes in. It's like being a superhero host, making sure guests feel right at home.

- **Warm Welcomes:** *Hachnasat Orchim* is about more than just throwing a party. It's about creating a warm and friendly atmosphere for anyone who walks through your door. It's like spreading kindness and hospitality like confetti!

- **Golden Rule:** Treating others the way you'd like to be treated is the golden rule of *Hachnasat Orchim*. It's like saying, "I want people to make me feel welcome when I visit, so I'm going to do the same for them."

### And in this superhero journey,

> *Hachnasat Orchim is all about being a superhero host, making others feel special, and turning every gathering into a warm and friendly celebration!*

# Heroes Among Us — Think

Heroes come in all shapes and sizes. They inspire us, showing that even in challenging times, one person can make a difference. Let's learn from some incredible heroes whose actions embody Jewish values.

## Abraham

Get ready for a journey into the past to meet Abraham Avinu, the trailblazer of faith and the very first Jewish patriarch. Imagine a time when many people believed in lots of gods, but not Abraham! He was like a superhero pioneer, boldly declaring, **"There's only one God, and I believe in one God."** Unlike those who came before him, like Adam and Eve or Noah, Abraham is the celebrated patriarch who set the stage for the Jewish people's unique journey into the belief in one God, also known as monotheism.

**Abraham and the Three Angels, watercolor by James Tissot, c. 1896–1902**

Now, let's dive into a captivating chapter of Abraham's life that showcases his unwavering faith and exceptional hospitality. Get ready for an inspiring adventure as we explore the remarkable story of Abraham and the Three Guests!

**The Jewish value that would fit Abraham is Faith and Welcoming guests**

Abraham Avinu wasn't a cape-wearing hero, but a warm-hearted one with a tent! No fancy suit, just simple clothes, yet he made a big impact. He didn't need a cape; all he needed was kindness and faith in one God. Pretty cool, right?

**The Story of Abraham and the Three Guests - A Cool Adventure with Surprise Guests**

*"Adonai appeared to Abraham near the great trees of Mamre while he was sitting at the entrance to his tent in the heat of the day. Abraham looked up and saw three men standing nearby."* (Genesis 18)

Instead of just saying hi, Abraham did something awesome – he invited them into his tent and treated them like VIPs! He gave them water to wash their feet, a comfy place to rest, and a super tasty meal. While they were enjoying the food, they told Abraham that his wife Sarah would have a baby, even though they were quite old. That's a big surprise, right?! Little did he know, these were not regular people; they were actually angels sent by God!

# Say BEcome a Hero

Remember, Heroes come in all shapes and sizes. They inspire us, showing that even in challenging times, one person can make a difference.

## You have the power to be a hero in your own life!

**Abraham Avinu**, a hero of Faith and Hospitality. Abraham Avinu's story is a timeless lesson in hospitality, faith, and the unexpected blessings that come from extending kindness to others. Just as Abraham opened his tent to strangers, let's strive to be hospitable and embrace life's surprises with faith and joy.

*Hachnasat Orchim*

**1. Recall a moment when you welcomed someone warmly. How did it make you feel?**

_____
_____

**2. Describe a situation where you could have been more welcoming. What would you do differently next time?.**

_____
_____

**3. Think about the power of hospitality. How can a small act of kindness, like offering a drink, make a difference?**

_____
_____

# BEcome a Hero — Say

**4. Have you ever been in a situation where you felt like a stranger? How did you wish to be treated?**

_____
_____
_____
_____

**5. Share a story of a time when you were a guest at someone's home. What made you feel welcome and comfortable?**

_____
_____
_____
_____

**6. Consider a community project to promote hospitality. How can you involve others in creating a welcoming environment? Share your plans.**

_____
_____
_____
_____

**You have the power to be a hero in your own life!**

# BEcome a Hero — To-Do-List

Guess what, heroes don't keep the lessons to themselves; they share it with the world.

## Teach & Inspire Others — *Hachnasat Orchim* — WELCOMING GUESTS

**Our Weekly Mitzvah:** Every Friday night, we have a special mitzvah called: *Kabbalat Shabbat*. It's like throwing a welcoming party for Shabbat, our day of rest every Saturday. Let's make it extra special by welcoming Shabbat with family and friend!

**Invite Family / Friends:**
Share a delicious Shabbat meal with your loved ones.

**Light two Shabbat Candles:**
Recite the blessing: *"Baruch Atah Adonai, Eloheinu Melech ha-olam, asher kid'shanu b'mitzvotav v'tzivanu l'hadlik ner shel Shabbat."*

בָּרוּךְ אַתָּה, יְיָ אֱלֹהֵינוּ, מֶלֶךְ הָעוֹלָם, אֲשֶׁר קִדְּשָׁנוּ בְּמִצְוֹתָיו, וְצִוָּנוּ לְהַדְלִיק נֵר שֶׁל שַׁבָּת.

Blessed are You, Adonai our God, Sovereign of the universe, who has sanctified us with Your commandments and commanded us to light the Shabbat candles.

**Bless the Grape Juice:** Pour grape juice into the Kiddush cup. Recite the Kiddush blessing over the grape juice: *"Baruch Atah Adonai, Eloheinu Melech ha-olam, borei p'ri hagafen."*

בָּרוּךְ אַתָּה, יְיָ אֱלֹהֵינוּ, מֶלֶךְ הָעוֹלָם, בּוֹרֵא פְּרִי הַגָּפֶן

Blessed are You, Adonai our God, Sovereign of the universe, who creates the fruit of the vine.

**Netilat Yadayim:** Recite the Kiddush blessing for washing hands *"Baruch Atah Adonai, Eloheinu Melech ha-olam, asher kid'shanu b'mitzvotav v'tzivanu al Netilat Yadayim."*

בָּרוּךְ אַתָּה ה' אֱלֹהֵינוּ מֶלֶךְ הָעוֹלָם אֲשֶׁר קִדְּשָׁנוּ בְּמִצְוֹתָיו וְצִוָּנוּ עַל נְטִילַת יָדַיִם

Blessed are You, Adonai our God, Sovereign of the universe, who has sanctified us with Your commandments and commanded us regarding the washing of hands.

**Make or buy two challahs:** the special braided bread for Shabbat. Recite the blessing over the challah: *"Baruch Atah Adonai, Eloheinu Melech ha-olam, hamotzi lechem min ha'aretz."*

בָּרוּךְ אַתָּה, יְיָ אֱלֹהֵינוּ, מֶלֶךְ הָעוֹלָם הַמּוֹצִיא לֶחֶם מִן הָאָרֶץ

Blessed are You, Adonai our God, Sovereign of all, who brings forth bread from the earth.

**\*Challah Recipe,** The Ingredients: flour, yeast, water, sugar, salt, eggs, and a bit of love. Mix, knead, let it rise, shape into a braid, and bake. Enjoy!

By following these steps, you're not just observing a mitzvah; you're mastering welcoming and hospitality, just like our patriarch Abraham!

# Middot & Mitzvot fun quiz!

**Here are five questions with multiple-choice answers:**

**Question 1: What is the essence of *Hachnasat Orchim*?**

A. Hosting parties every day
B. Treating guests with kindness and warmth
C. Ignoring visitors
D. Closing doors to strangers

**Question 2: How can you practice the Mitzvah of *Hachnasat Orchim* in your daily life?**

A. By avoiding talking to others
B. By offering a warm welcome to guests
C. By keeping all your belongings to yourself
D. By never inviting friends over

**Question 3: Which character trait aligns with the concept of *Hachnasat Orchim*?**

A. Ignoring newcomers
B. Seeking and pursuing hospitality
C. Creating barriers for guests
D. Hiding from social interactions

**Question 4: What can we learn from the story of Abraham and the three visitors?**

A. Ignoring guests is acceptable
B. Welcoming strangers is a noble act
C. Never share food with others
D. Hospitality has no value in Judaism

**Question 5: Why is *Hachnasat Orchim* considered an important value in Judaism?**

A. It's a secret code for Jewish families
B. It's a superhero's special power
C. It promotes kindness, warmth, and openness
D. It's a popular Jewish song title

(Answers on p. 151)

# Chapter Two

Shalom (Peace)
Rodef Shalom (Pursuing Peace)

# PEACE
HI, BYE

# Shalom

**PURSUING PEACE**  Rodef Shalom  רוֹדֵף שָׁלוֹם

*Shalom*, the Jewish idea of peace, and *Rodef Shalom*, the idea of working for peace, are like being a superhero with a special puzzle piece for making things peaceful.

It's like having a superpower to bring calm to our lives and the world around us.

Think of holding a puzzle piece that helps make everything work together smoothly. *Shalom* and *Rodef Shalom* want us to be peace superheroes, using our special piece to build connections and make friends. We become champions of making things peaceful.

*Rodef Shalom* is all about working for peace. It's like being a peace detective – someone who tries to make things better and happier. Just imagine spreading peace everywhere, just like sunshine! That's how important it is!

"Imagine all the people living life in peace."  – John Lennon

# How are you feeling today?

Date: _____

# My Mitzvot & Middot Weekly Journal

Describe your mood at this moment with a word/emoji. Circle the word that fits best.

_____  Happy  Loving  Curious  Grateful  Surprised  Sad  Inspired  Nervous  Bored

## Mitzvot Tracker

Which mitzvot did you perform this week? Check off the Mitzvot and/or write your own.

- [ ] Donated to charity.
- [ ] Helped a neighbor.
- [ ] Prayed at the synagogue.
- [ ] Volunteered at a community event.
- [ ] Respected others.
- [ ] Visited someone who is sick.
- [ ] Followed Shabbat rituals.
- [ ] Shared food with someone in need.
- [ ] Fed and played with my pet
- [ ] Studied Jewish text.

## Middot Tracker

Reflect on your interactions with others

**Check off the Middot you've practiced this week**

- [ ] **Kindness:** Helped a friend.
- [ ] **Honesty:** Admitted a mistake.
- [ ] **Patience:** Waited for a turn without getting upset.
- [ ] **Respect:** Listened attentively to others.
- [ ] **Compassion:** Comforted a friend in need.
- [ ] **Responsibility:** Completed chores without being asked.
- [ ] **Gratitude:** Thanked someone for their help.
- [ ] **Humility:** Accepted constructive criticism gracefully.
- [ ] **Courage:** Spoke up against unfairness.
- [ ] **Forgiveness:** Pardoned someone for a mistake.

Write down your own if it's not listed

# PEACE

## *More on* Shalom

- **World Peace Puzzle:** Embracing *Shalom* and *Rodef Shalom* transforms us into peace superheroes with a global vision. Our puzzle piece adds to the bigger picture of harmony, making us ambassadors of peace.

- **Bridge Builder:** *Shalom* and *Rodef Shalom* serve as the puzzle piece for building bridges. With it, we mend relationships, resolve conflicts, and foster unity. As peace superheroes, we spread peace and understanding.

- **Symphony of Serenity:** As superheroes of *Shalom* and *Rodef Shalom*, we celebrate diversity, creating a mosaic of peace. Our peace puzzle piece symbolizes our shared humanity.

- **Peace Catalyst:** *Shalom* and *Rodef Shalom* catalyze peace, inspiring kindness, compassion, and understanding. We use our puzzle piece to nurture positive relationships within our community, becoming superheroes of peace.

**And in this superhero journey,**

*Shalom* and *Rodef Shalom* transform us into superheroes of peace. It's like having a puzzle piece that symbolizes our commitment to creating a world filled with harmony and understanding. Our superhero puzzle piece inspires others to join the puzzle of peace, one piece at a time. How peaceful is that?

# Heroes Among Us *Think*

Heroes come in all shapes and sizes. They inspire us, showing that even in challenging times, one person can make a difference. Let's learn from some incredible heroes whose actions embody Jewish values.

**Itzhak Rabin** Former Prime Minister of Israel, Nobel Peace Prize winner, worked towards peace in the Middle East. Now, he wasn't a superhero in a cape, but he did something amazing for the Jewish people.

- **Peace Warrior:** Rabin was like a peace superhero! He believed that people could solve problems by talking instead of fighting. It's like having a superhero who uses words instead of punches.

- **Soldier Turned Leader:** Before becoming a leader, Rabin was a brave soldier. He even helped Israel win an important war! Later, he decided to use his courage for peace and became the Prime Minister of Israel.

- **Oslo Accords:** Rabin played a big role in making an agreement called the Oslo Accords. It was like a superhero team-up but with countries, where Israel and Palestine agreed to work towards peace. Rabin led the way, using words instead of weapons to unite people who saw each other as enemies.

So, Itzhak Rabin wasn't a hero who wore a cape, but he was a hero in a uniform and later in a suit, using his courage and leadership to bring peace to the Jewish people.

**The Jewish value that would fit Itzhak Rabin is *Rodef Shalom* (Pursuing Peace)**

One day, someone asked Itzhak Rabin why he worked so hard for peace. With a wise smile, he explained, "Pursuing peace, or Rodef Shalom, is like being a superhero for your people. It's about stopping fights and making sure everyone can live happily together." Itzhak Rabin believed that pursuing peace was the most heroic thing a person could do.

Itzhak Rabin had a history as a brave soldier, defending his country with courage. One day, he realized that true strength lies in bringing people together, not in fighting against them. It was like discovering a new kind of superhero power - the ability to create peace. And so, Itzhak Rabin became a real-life superhero, not with a cape, but with a vision for a world where everyone could live in harmony.

So, when we talk about *Rodef Shalom,* we remember the hero who dedicated his life to pursuing peace, just like superheroes fighting for a better world. Super cool, indeed!

# Say ♥ BEcome a Hero

Remember, Heroes come in all shapes and sizes. They inspire us, showing that even in challenging times, one person can make a difference.

## You have the power to be a hero in your own life!

**Yitzhak Rabin**, a hero of *Rodef Shalom*. Rabin worked hard to bring peace between Israelis and Palestinians. He once said, "**You don't make peace with friends. You make it with very unsavory enemies.**" This means he believed in talking to even those who disagreed to find common ground. Rabin's dedication to peace, even when it was tough, shows us the power of understanding. He inspires us to work towards a world where everyone can live together in harmony, emphasizing the importance of peace, empathy, and positive change.

1. Recall a moment when you did something kind for someone else.
What did you learn from that experience? How did it make you feel?

_____

_____

2. Describe a situation where you helped bring positivity to a gloomy day. It could be for a friend, family member, or even yourself.

_____

_____

3. Think about the power of '*Shalom*' or '*Rodef Shalom*.'
What small thing can you do today to bring peace to your surroundings?

_____

_____

 # BEcome a Hero

**4. Describe a time when you helped make peace between friends.**

_____
_____
_____
_____

**5. Share a situation where you chose kindness over conflict.**

_____
_____
_____
_____

**6. Consider a group or community project you could initiate to promote harmony. What steps would you take to make it happen? Share your plans.**

_____
_____
_____
_____

**You have the power to be a hero in your own life!**

# BEcome a Hero — To-Do-List

Guess what, heroes don't keep the lessons to themselves; they share it with the world.

## Teach & Inspire Others  *Shalom*

**Choose one or more actions to inspire others and spread the lessons of PEACE & HARMONY**

**Create a Peace Poster:**
- <u>Example:</u> Use a large poster board. Draw a diverse group of people holding hands.
- Write, "Together We Build Peace" "Spread Love" and "Be a Friend" in bold letters.
- Add colorful peace symbols and positive affirmations.

**Write a Peaceful Poem:**
- <u>Example:</u> Write a poem titled "Whispers of Peace" or "Harmony in Our Hearts."
- Express feelings of unity and understanding.
- Use metaphors like "bridges of kindness" or "garden of empathy."

**Peaceful Presentation:**
- <u>Example:</u> Create a PowerPoint presentation titled "Building Bridges to Peace."
- Include images of Yitzhak Rabin and his quotes.
- Speak about your own experiences with pursuing peace.
- Conclude with a call to action for the audience.

**Kindness Challenge:**
- <u>Example:</u> Develop a "Week of Kindness" checklist.
- Include tasks like "Smile at a stranger", "Help a classmate/a teacher."
- Design a visually appealing checklist and distribute copies to classmates.

**Storytime for Peace:**
- <u>Example:</u> Write a story titled "The Puzzle of Friendship."
- Depict characters solving a puzzle together, symbolizing collaboration.
- Illustrate moments of understanding and compromise.
- Share the story with classmates, emphasizing the value of working together.

Remember, by completing one of these actions, you're actively contributing to a more peaceful and harmonious environment. Let's take these small steps together to make a big difference!"

# Middot & Mitzvot fun quiz!

### Here are five questions with multiple-choice answers:

**Question 1: What is the meaning of *Shalom*?**

A. A type of Jewish dance
B. A greeting meaning peace
C. A special holiday tradition
D. A type of Jewish song

**Question 2: How can you practice the Middah (value) of *Shalom* in your daily life?**

A. By telling jokes all the time
B. By avoiding talking to others
C. By being kind and making peace with friends
D. By keeping all your toys to yourself

**Question 3: Which Mitzvah aligns with the concept of *Rodef Shalom*?**

A. Ignoring conflicts and walking away
B. Seeking and pursuing peace
C. Creating chaos and arguments
D. Hiding from difficult situations

**Question 4: What is a significant event associated with Yitzhak Rabin, reflecting the value of *Rodef Shalom*?**

A. Winning a Nobel Prize in Literature
B. Signing a peace agreement with Palestinians
C. Inventing a new type of technology
D. Hosting an international cooking show

**Question 5: Why is *Rodef Shalom* considered an important value in Judaism?**

A. Because it's a secret code for Jewish families
B. Because it's a superhero's special power
C. Because it's a quality that brings harmony and goodness
D. Because it's a popular Jewish song title

(Answers on p. 151)

# Chapter Three

Din (Justice)
Rachamim (Mercy)

# JUSTICE / MERCY  ③ דִּין / רַחֲמִים

## Din / Rachamim

Did you know that *Din* is about following the rules and ensuring that everyone receives what they deserve? Upholding justice contributes to fairness and equality in society.

Did you know that *Rachamim* is about showing compassion and not treating others harshly, even when they may deserve it?

Practicing mercy fosters understanding and empathy, promoting a more compassionate and harmonious world.

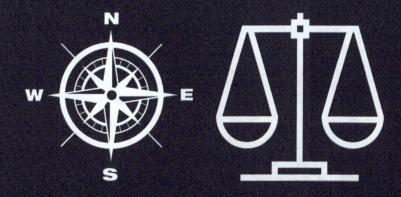

# How are You feeling today?

Date: _____

# My Mitzvot & Middot Weekly Journal

Describe your mood at this moment with a word/emoji.  Circle the word that fits best.

_____  Happy  Loving  Curious  Grateful  Surprised  Sad  Inspired  Nervous  Bored

## Mitzvot Tracker

**Which mitzvot did you perform this week? Check off the Mitzvot and/or write your own.**

- [ ] Donated to charity.
- [ ] Helped a neighbor.
- [ ] Prayed at the synagogue.
- [ ] Volunteered at a community event.
- [ ] Respected others.
- [ ] Visited someone who is sick.
- [ ] Followed Shabbat rituals.
- [ ] Shared food with someone in need.
- [ ] Fed and played with my pet
- [ ] Studied Jewish text.

## Middot Tracker

**Reflect on your interactions with others**

**Check off the Middot you've practiced this week**

- [ ] **Kindness:** Helped a friend.
- [ ] **Honesty:** Admitted a mistake.
- [ ] **Patience:** Waited for a turn without getting upset.
- [ ] **Respect:** Listened attentively to others.
- [ ] **Compassion:** Comforted a friend in need.
- [ ] **Responsibility:** Completed chores without being asked.
- [ ] **Gratitude:** Thanked someone for their help.
- [ ] **Humility:** Accepted constructive criticism gracefully.
- [ ] **Courage:** Spoke up against unfairness.
- [ ] **Forgiveness:** Pardoned someone for a mistake.

**Write down your own if it's not listed**

# JUSTICE / MERCY    דִּין / רַחֲמִים

## More on Din / Rachamim

- **Balancing Scales:** *Din* and *Rachamim* are like two sides of the same coin. Din represents justice, making sure things are fair and right. It's like a scale, keeping everything in balance. On the other hand, Rachamim is all about mercy, offering compassion and understanding, even when strict justice might say otherwise.

- **Guiding Compass:** Just like a compass helps you find your way, *Din/Rachamim* guides us in making decisions. It's like having a moral compass that points us toward fairness and kindness. Sometimes, we need the strictness of *Din*, and other times, the compassion of *Rachamim* lights our path.

- **Harmony of Values:** *Din / Rachamim* teaches us to find harmony between justice and mercy. It's like a melody where both notes play together beautifully, creating a song of fairness and compassion in our actions and decisions.

### And in this superhero journey,

> *Din / Rachamim* is like having a compass that helps us navigate the complex terrain of justice and mercy, ensuring our actions are both fair and compassionate. How incredible is that?

# Heroes Among Us  *Think*

Heroes come in all shapes and sizes. They inspire us, showing that even in challenging times, one person can make a difference. Let's learn from some incredible heroes whose actions embody Jewish values.

## King Solomon

King Solomon, a prolific author, wise judge, and visionary architect, played a pivotal role in shaping ancient Israel. Renowned for his wisdom, he authored biblical books like Proverbs and Ecclesiastes, offering timeless insights. As a fair judge, he famously resolved disputes, including the well-known baby-splitting incident. Solomon's architectural legacy includes overseeing the construction of the First Temple in Jerusalem, a symbol of divine presence. His multifaceted contributions solidify his influence on literature, justice, and the cultural heritage of Israel.

**Solomon's Wealth and Wisdom 1896**

### Solomon's Wise Verdict: The Baby-Splitting Judgment

Once, two women approached King Solomon with a baby, each claiming to be the child's mother. Unable to determine the true mother, Solomon devised a clever solution. He proposed to divide the baby in half, giving each woman half of the child. One woman readily agreed, while the other begged Solomon to spare the baby's life and give it to the other woman. Solomon, recognizing the true mother's selflessness and love, declared her the real parent and granted her custody of the baby. The wise judgment revealed the depth of a mother's love and showcased Solomon's renowned wisdom.

**Judgement of Solomon by DORÉ, Gustave 1865**

### King Solomon, The Queen of Sheba, and the Bee Tale

Once upon a time, King Solomon sat on his golden throne, surrounded by his wise men. The Queen of Sheba entered with a challenge. In her hands, she held two flowers—one from Solomon's garden and the other crafted by a skilled artist. The king, famed for his wisdom, faced a puzzling choice. Unable to distinguish between the real, and the fake flower, Solomon cleverly called for a window to be opened. Bees, drawn to the sweet flowers outside, entered the room. Without hesitation, they buzzed to the flower from Solomon's garden, ignoring the artificial one. In that moment, King Solomon revealed his wisdom, saying, "O Queen of Sheba, the bees have given you my answer." And the queen said, "You are wise, King Solomon. You gather knowledge from the little things which common men pass by unnoticed."

**The Jewish value that would fit King Solomon is wisdom, Justice & Compassion**

# Say BEcome a Hero

Remember, Heroes come in all shapes and sizes. They inspire us, showing that even in challenging times, one person can make a difference.

## You have the power to be a hero in your own life!

**King Solomon,** in the rich tapestry of biblical history, emerges as a figure not only renowned for his wisdom but also for his understanding of justice (*Din*) and compassion (*Rachamim*). His stories, particularly the famous tale of the baby-splitting and the encounter with the bees, provide profound insights into navigating the delicate balance between justice and compassion. Let's explore these narratives, reflect on our own choices, and develop the qualities that can transform us into heroes mastering *Din* and *Rachamim.*

**1. Reflect on a situation where you had to make a fair decision.
How did you feel, and what guided your choice?**

_____

_____

**2. Consider a time when you showed compassion to someone who needed it.
How did it make a difference?**

_____

_____

**3. Think about the balance between justice (*Din*) and compassion (*Rachamim*).
When is it important to be just, and when is compassion needed?**

_____

_____

**4. Share a personal or fictional story where someone demonstrated both justice and compassion. What can we learn from such stories?**

_____

_____

_____

_____

**5. Reflect on King Solomon's wisdom in the story of baby-splitting. How can this tale guide you in making fair decisions in your own life?**

_____

_____

_____

_____

**6. Consider a community project to promote justice and mercy. How can you involve others in creating an environment that values fairness and compassion? Share your plans.**

_____

_____

_____

_____

**You have the power to be a hero in your own life!**

Guess what, heroes don't keep the lessons to themselves; they share it with the world.

## Teach & Inspire Others  *Din/Rachamim*

**Choose one or more actions to inspire others and spread the lessons of JUSTICE (*Din*) & COMPASSION (*Rachamim*)**

**Fairness Journal:**
- Start a journal to write about situations where fairness is important.
- Think about how you can make fair choices.
- Consider the impact of your actions on others.

**Empathy Challenge:**
- Challenge yourself to understand how others feel.
- When a friend is upset, listen and try to see things from their perspective.
- Think about how you would want to be treated.

**Sharing Circle:**
- Gather friends or family for a sharing circle.
- Share stories of times when fairness made a positive impact.
- Discuss how acts of kindness can create a compassionate community.

**Conflict Resolution Practice:**
- Practice resolving conflicts peacefully.
- Learn to express your thoughts without hurting others.
- Understand that finding common ground is a step toward compassion.

**Random Acts of Compassion:**
- Look for chances to show kindness without being asked.
- Help a classmate who is struggling.
- Be a friend to someone who might feel left out.

**Justice and compassion go hand in hand. By making fair choices and showing kindness, you contribute to a more just and compassionate world!**

# Middot & Mitzvot fun quiz!

**Here are five questions with multiple-choice answers:**

**Question 1: What does the term *Din* refer to in Jewish teachings?**

A. Justice and Fairness
B. Mercy and Compassion
C. Joy and Celebration
D. Wisdom and Knowledge

**Question 2: When is *Rachamim* most likely to be emphasized?**

A. During times of celebration
B. When making fair decisions
C. In moments of compassion and mercy
D. In the pursuit of knowledge

**Question 3: How does the story of King Solomon's baby-splitting showcase the concept of *Din*?**

A. By emphasizing the importance of compassion
B. By illustrating the challenge of making just decisions
C. By highlighting the joy of fairness
D. By showcasing the wisdom of compromise

**Question 4: In which situation is *Rachamim* more applicable?**

A. Solving a complex problem with fairness
B. Showing kindness and compassion to others
C. Making a decision based on strict justice
D. Celebrating achievements and success

**Question 5: Which Jewish value aligns closely with the balance of *Din* and *Rachamim*?**

A. *Tzedakah* (Charity)
B. *Kavod* (Respect)
C. *Chesed* (Kindness)
D. *Emunah* (Faith)

(Answers on p. 151)

# Chapter Four

Teshuvah (Repentance)

# REPENTANCE

## Teshuvah

Did you know that *Teshuvah* is like having a reset button for the soul? *Teshuvah* allows us to reflect, learn, and grow, ensuring that we continuously strive to be the best version of ourselves.

How amazing is that?

# How are You feeling today?

Date: _____

# My Mitzvot & Middot Weekly Journal

Describe your mood at this moment with a word/emoji.  Circle the word that fits best.

_____ Happy  Loving  Curious  Grateful  Surprised  Sad  Inspired  Nervous  Bored

## Mitzvot Tracker

Which mitzvot did you perform this week? Check off the Mitzvot and/or write your own.

- [ ] Donated to charity.
- [ ] Helped a neighbor.
- [ ] Prayed at the synagogue.
- [ ] Volunteered at a community event.
- [ ] Respected others.
- [ ] Visited someone who is sick.
- [ ] Followed Shabbat rituals.
- [ ] Shared food with someone in need.
- [ ] Fed and played with my pet
- [ ] Studied Jewish text.

## Middot Tracker

Reflect on your interactions with others

**Check off the Middot you've practiced this week**

- [ ] **Kindness:** Helped a friend.
- [ ] **Honesty:** Admitted a mistake.
- [ ] **Patience:** Waited for a turn without getting upset.
- [ ] **Respect:** Listened attentively to others.
- [ ] **Compassion:** Comforted a friend in need.
- [ ] **Responsibility:** Completed chores without being asked.
- [ ] **Gratitude:** Thanked someone for their help.
- [ ] **Humility:** Accepted constructive criticism gracefully.
- [ ] **Courage:** Spoke up against unfairness.
- [ ] **Forgiveness:** Pardoned someone for a mistake.

Write down your own if it's not listed

# REPENTANCE

## More on Teshuvah

- **A Fresh Start:** *Teshuvah* is a powerful concept that allows us to make amends and start fresh. It's like having a reset button that gives us the chance to learn from our mistakes and become better individuals.

- **Reflect and Return:** *Teshuvah* involves reflecting on our actions, realizing where we may have gone wrong, and committing to change. It's a journey of self-improvement and returning to our best selves.

- **Mending Relationships:** Just as a heartfelt apology can mend relationships, *Teshuvah* helps repair our connection with God and others. It's about acknowledging mistakes, seeking forgiveness, and rebuilding trust.

- **Courage to Change:** *Teshuvah* requires courage to face our shortcomings and take the necessary steps to change. It's a process of personal growth and transformation, demonstrating resilience in the face of our imperfections.

### And in this superhero journey,

> *Teshuvah is like having a reset button for the soul, allowing us to reflect, learn, and grow, ensuring that we continuously strive to be the best version of ourselves. How amazing is that?*

# Heroes Among Us — Think

Heroes come in all shapes and sizes. They inspire us, showing that even in challenging times, one person can make a difference. Let's learn from some incredible heroes whose actions embody Jewish values.

## Jonah:
### A Heroic Journey of Choices

Long ago, in the land of Israel, there lived a man named Jonah. He was a special person because he was chosen by God to be a prophet.

**Now, you might wonder, what's a prophet?** Well, a prophet is someone who speaks for God. They receive messages from God and share them with others. Sometimes these messages are about what people need to do to be better or to avoid something bad happening. Jonah was one of these prophets.

Jonah and the Whale (1621) by Pieter Lastman

One day, God gave him a very important job. He was supposed to go to a city called Nineveh and tell the people there to stop being mean and start being good.

But Jonah didn't want to do it. He was scared and ran away instead. As he tried to escape on a ship, a huge storm came. The sailors were afraid, and they found out Jonah was the reason for the storm. So, Jonah told them to throw him overboard to stop it. And that's when something incredible happened – a giant fish swallowed Jonah!

Inside the fish, Jonah realized he made a mistake, you cant really run away from God, God is everywhere. He prayed and asked for forgiveness. After three days, the fish spit him out onto dry land.

Jonah then did what God asked him to do. He went to Nineveh and told the people to change their ways. Surprisingly, they listened, and the city was saved from destruction.

Jonah's story is a timeless tale of the heroic journey we all undertake in life. It reminds us that heroes are not perfect; they make mistakes but have the power to choose *Teshuvah* (Repentance), to turn away from wrongdoing and towards a better path.

In the end, it's the journey of learning from our errors that makes us truly heroic. Jonah's narrative also emphasizes the significance of second chances and the importance of following what's right, even when it's difficult.

**Did you know?** We revisit Jonah's story from the Bible every year on *Yom Kippur*, the holiest day in the Jewish calendar, to remind us of these valuable lessons.

# Say BEcome a Hero

Remember, Heroes come in all shapes and sizes. They inspire us, showing that even in challenging times, one person can make a difference.

## You have the power to be a hero in your own life!

**1. Reflect on a time in your life when you recognized a mistake. How did you feel, and what steps did you take to make amends?**

_____

_____

_____

**2. Consider a situation where you might have hurt someone unintentionally. How would you approach them to seek forgiveness and repair the relationship?**

_____

_____

_____

**3. *Teshuvah* involves both acknowledging wrongdoings and committing to positive change. What are some actionable steps you can take to demonstrate genuine repentance?**

_____

_____

_____

**4. Think about a challenging decision you've made. How did the concept of *Teshuvah* influence your choices and actions?**

_____
_____
_____
_____

**5. In Jonah's story, we see the potential for redemption and growth. How can *Teshuvah* inspire personal growth and development in your own life?**

_____
_____
_____
_____

**6. Imagine a scenario where someone seeks forgiveness from you. How would you approach the situation, and what factors would you consider in deciding whether to offer forgiveness?**

_____
_____
_____
_____

**You have the power to be a hero in your own life!**

# BEcome a Hero To-Do-List

Guess what, heroes don't keep the lessons to themselves; they share it with the world.

## Teach & Inspire Others — Teshuvah

**Choose one or more actions to inspire others and spread the lessons of REPENTANCE and RETURN**

### Reflective Journaling:
- Start a diary to jot down your thoughts and actions.
- Think about times you could have done better.
- Consider how you can improve next time.

### Kindness Calendar:
- Use a calendar and do one small act of kindness each day.
- Day 1: Say something nice to a friend.
- Day 5: Help a classmate with their homework.

### Storytelling Share Circle:
- Gather friends or family for a storytelling circle.
- Share stories of positive change and growth.
- Narrate a story about learning from mistakes.

### Problem-Solving Challenge:
- Challenge yourself to solve problems in a positive way.
- Practice talking openly and understanding others.
- Learn to resolve disagreements without arguing.

### Random Acts of *Teshuvah*:
- Look for chances to apologize or make things right.
- If you accidentally hurt someone's feelings, say sorry.
- Even small efforts create a more positive environment.

**Remember:** *Teshuvah* is about learning, growing, and making the world a better place. Each small step brings you closer to a kinder and more thoughtful future!

# Middot & Mitzvot fun quiz!

**Here are five questions with multiple-choice answers:**

**Question 1: What does the term *Teshuvah* mean in Judaism?**

A. Celebration of achievements
B. Repentance and return
C. Wisdom and knowledge
D. Charity and kindness

**Question 2: When is *Teshuvah* typically emphasized in the Jewish calendar?**
A. During festive celebrations
B. In moments of personal success
C. In the month of Elul and the Ten Days of Repentance
D. Randomly throughout the year

**Question 3: What is the primary goal of *Teshuvah*?**

A. To accumulate material wealth
B. To seek revenge on others
C. To acknowledge mistakes and seek forgiveness
D. To ignore personal shortcomings

**Question 4: How does *Teshuvah* differ from a simple apology?**

A. *Teshuvah* involves seeking forgiveness only from oneself.
B. An apology focuses on blaming others for one's actions.
C. *Teshuvah* requires acknowledging mistakes and making amends.
D. Apologies are unnecessary in the process of *Teshuvah*.

**Question 5: How does *Teshuvah* contribute to personal growth and development?**

A. By ignoring mistakes and moving forward
B. By blaming others for one's actions
C. By acknowledging wrongdoings and seeking positive change
D. By avoiding responsibility for one's choices

(Answers on p. 151)

# Chapter Five

Emunah (Faith)

# FAITH

## Emunah

*Emunah* is like a sturdy anchor for the soul. *Emunah* is our superhero faith, guiding us with trust and belief in the unseen, making our journey through life meaningful. It provides stability, strength, and trust as we navigate the seas of life.

How incredible is that?

# How are You feeling today?

Date: _____

# My Mitzvot & Middot Weekly Journal

Describe your mood at this moment with a word/emoji. Circle the word that fits best.

_____  Happy  Loving  Curious  Grateful  Surprised  Sad  Inspired  Nervous  Bored

## Mitzvot Tracker

Which mitzvot did you perform this week? Check off the Mitzvot and/or write your own.

- [ ] Donated to charity.
- [ ] Helped a neighbor.
- [ ] Prayed at the synagogue.
- [ ] Volunteered at a community event.
- [ ] Respected others.
- [ ] Visited someone who is sick.
- [ ] Followed Shabbat rituals.
- [ ] Shared food with someone in need.
- [ ] Fed and played with my pet
- [ ] Studied Jewish text.

## Middot Tracker

Reflect on your interactions with others

**Check off the Middot you've practiced this week**

- [ ] **Kindness:** Helped a friend.
- [ ] **Honesty:** Admitted a mistake.
- [ ] **Patience:** Waited for a turn without getting upset.
- [ ] **Respect:** Listened attentively to others.
- [ ] **Compassion:** Comforted a friend in need.
- [ ] **Responsibility:** Completed chores without being asked.
- [ ] **Gratitude:** Thanked someone for their help.
- [ ] **Humility:** Accepted constructive criticism gracefully.
- [ ] **Courage:** Spoke up against unfairness.
- [ ] **Forgiveness:** Pardoned someone for a mistake.

Write down your own if it's not listed

# FAITH

## *More on* Emunah

- **Faith as an Anchor:** *Emunah* is a powerful concept in Judaism that acts as a firm anchor for our souls. It provides a sense of stability and trust, even in the face of life's uncertainties.

- **Belief in the Unseen:** *Emunah* is all about believing in things we may not see directly. It's like having confidence in the sunrise even when the sky is still dark. It encourages us to trust in God and have faith in the unseen aspects of life.

- **Strength in Adversity:** Just as a strong anchor keeps a ship steady during a storm, *Emunah* gives us strength during challenging times. It's a source of comfort, reminding us that we are not alone and that there's a guiding force in our lives.

- **Building Trust:** *Emunah* involves building a deep trust in God and the path set before us. It's about recognizing that challenges are part of a greater plan and that our faith can guide us through every twist and turn.

### And in this superhero journey,

*Emunah* is like a sturdy anchor for the soul, providing stability, strength, and trust as we navigate the seas of life. How incredible is that?

# Heroes Among Us — Think

Heroes come in all shapes and sizes. They inspire us, showing that even in challenging times, one person can make a difference. Let's learn from some incredible heroes whose actions embody Jewish values.

## Moses

Moses wasn't your usual leader. He didn't feel super confident, and he wasn't sure if anyone would listen to him. But you know what? He had faith—faith in something bigger than himself. Born during a time when the Pharaoh ordered the death of Hebrew male infants, Moses' mother courageously placed him in a basket, floating him down the Nile. Adopted by Pharaoh's daughter, Moses lived a privileged life in the Egyptian royal court until he discovered his Hebrew heritage.

The Finding of Moses, by Sir Lawrence Alma-Tadema, 1904

At the age of 40, Moses witnessed an injustice and, driven by his sense of justice, fled Egypt. For the next 40 years, he embraced a simple life as a shepherd, learning valuable lessons of humility and empathy. At the age of 80, while tending his flock, Moses encountered the burning bush—an event that would mark the beginning of his transformative role in history.

### Moses and the Burning Bush

As Moses approached the burning bush, God spoke to him, revealing His plan to free the Israelites from slavery in Egypt. Despite initial hesitation, Moses, guided by his unwavering faith, accepted the monumental task. With his brother Aaron, he confronted Pharaoh, demanding the release of the Israelites. The ensuing journey through the desert lasted 40 years, during which Moses faced numerous challenges, displayed extraordinary leadership, and imparted invaluable teachings.

Moses with the Tablets of the Law – by Guido Reni, 1624

### Moses as Rabbi and Leader

Moses was our first rabbi (teacher). He shared the important rules and teachings that he received from God. Even though he knew he wasn't perfect, Moses was really humble and down-to-earth. He admitted his mistakes, showing everyone that it's okay to be imperfect. His time as a leader reached its peak when the Israelites finally reached the Promised Land. This was a special place that God had promised them. Moses led them through challenges and triumphs, always staying true to his faith and commitment to God's plan.

**Moses' life was a big journey**—from living in fancy royal courts to humble shepherd's fields, from encountering the burning bush to leading the Exodus (Passover story). At first, he wasn't so sure about being a leader, but he ended up becoming the one who shared God's commandments with the people. When Moses passed away at the age of 120, he left behind a powerful legacy of faith, leadership, and a strong commitment to the values that are important in Jewish heritage.

# Say ♥ BEcome a Hero

Remember, Heroes come in all shapes and sizes. They inspire us, showing that even in challenging times, one person can make a difference.

## You have the power to be a hero in your own life!

**Understanding *Emunah*:** *Emunah*, the Jewish concept of faith, is like having a strong belief in something even if you can't see it directly. Think about a time when you had to believe in something without seeing it.

**1. Think about a time when you had to believe in something without seeing it. How did it feel, and what helped you hold onto that belief?**

_____

_____

**2. Moses wasn't always super confident, but he had faith in God. Have you ever doubted yourself or felt unsure about something? How did you handle those moments, and what helped you keep going?**

_____

_____

**3. *Emunah* often involves trusting that there's a plan even when things seem tough. Reflect on a challenging situation you faced. How did the idea of trusting in a bigger plan help you navigate through it?**

_____

_____

# BEcome a Hero  *Say*

**4. Moses showed that faith can give you strength, even in difficult times. Can you think of a time when your faith or belief in something helped you find strength or courage?**

_____
_____
_____
_____

**5. *Emunah* isn't just for big moments; it can be part of everyday life. How can having faith in yourself and others make a difference in your daily experiences?**

_____
_____
_____
_____

**6. Moses shared his faith with the Israelites. If you were to share something you strongly believe in with others, what would it be, and how would you go about sharing it in a positive way?**

_____
_____
_____
_____

**You have the power to be a hero in your own life!**

Guess what, heroes don't keep the lessons to themselves; they share it with the world.

## Teach & Inspire Others — Emunah

**Choose one or more actions to inspire others and spread the lessons of FAITH**

**Gratitude Journal:**
- Start a journal to express thanks daily.
- Reflect on positive aspects of each day.

Example: Write about something you're grateful for each day, like a friend, family, or a moment that made you happy.

**Nature Connection - Bring it Home:**
- Collect nature items; create a small "faith corner."
- Use it for moments of faith reflection.

Example: Use rocks, leaves, or flowers to build a small corner. When you see it, take a moment to reflect on your faith.

**Story Sharing Circle:**
- Gather to share faith-inspired stories.
- Discuss moments when faith overcame challenges.

Example: Share a story about a time when your faith helped you overcome a challenge or made a tough situation easier.

**Mindful Moments:**
- Take quiet reflection breaks.
- Practice mindfulness for faith connection.

Example: Find a quiet spot, close your eyes, and take deep breaths. Use this time to connect with your faith.

**Faith Board:**
- Create a visual board with images or words that represent your faith.
- Update it regularly with new additions.

Example: Print out images or write words that symbolize your faith. Include quotes or verses that inspire you.

Approach these tasks with enthusiasm, knowing that each act will strengthen your connection to faith and contribute to positive growth!

# Middot & Mitzvot fun quiz!

### Here are five questions with multiple-choice answers:

**Question 1: What does the term *Emunah* refer to in Jewish teachings?**

A. Justice and Fairness
B. Mercy and Compassion
C. Trust and Faith
D. Wisdom and Knowledge

**Question 2: When is *Emunah* most likely to be emphasized?**

A. During times of celebration
B. When making fair decisions
C. In moments of compassion and mercy
D. In trusting the unseen and having faith

**Question 3: How does the concept of *Emunah* influence our understanding of life's challenges?**

A. By emphasizing the importance of compassion
B. By illustrating the challenge of making just decisions
C. By highlighting the joy of fairness
D. By encouraging trust and faith in the face of challenges

**Question 4: In which situation is *Emunah* more applicable?**

A. Solving a complex problem with fairness
B. Showing kindness and compassion to others
C. Making a decision based on strict justice
D. Trusting in a positive outcome despite uncertainties

**Question 5: Which Jewish value aligns closely with the essence of *Emunah*?**

A. *Tzedakah* (Charity)
B. *Kavod* (Respect)
C. *Chesed* (Kindness)
D. *Emunah* (Faith)

(Answers on p. 151)

# Chapter Six

Chaverut (Friendship)

# FRIENDSHIP

## Chaverut

Did you know that *Chaverut* is like having a treasure chest of friendships?

*Chaverut* is like - a collection of priceless gems that brighten our days and accompany us on life's incredible journey.

How wonderful is that?

# How are you feeling today?

Date: _____

# My Mitzvot & Middot Weekly Journal

Describe your mood at this moment with a word/emoji. Circle the word that fits best.

| _____ | Happy | Loving | Curious | Grateful | Surprised | Sad | Inspired | Nervous | Bored |

## Mitzvot Tracker

Which mitzvot did you perform this week? Check off the Mitzvot and/or write your own.

- ☐ Donated to charity.
- ☐ Helped a neighbor.
- ☐ Prayed at the synagogue.
- ☐ Volunteered at a community event.
- ☐ Respected others.
- ☐ Visited someone who is sick.
- ☐ Followed Shabbat rituals.
- ☐ Shared food with someone in need.
- ☐ Fed and played with my pet
- ☐ Studied Jewish text.

## Middot Tracker

**Reflect on your interactions with others**

**Check off the Middot you've practiced this week**

- ☐ **Kindness:** Helped a friend.
- ☐ **Honesty:** Admitted a mistake.
- ☐ **Patience:** Waited for a turn without getting upset.
- ☐ **Respect:** Listened attentively to others.
- ☐ **Compassion:** Comforted a friend in need.
- ☐ **Responsibility:** Completed chores without being asked.
- ☐ **Gratitude:** Thanked someone for their help.
- ☐ **Humility:** Accepted constructive criticism gracefully.
- ☐ **Courage:** Spoke up against unfairness.
- ☐ **Forgiveness:** Pardoned someone for a mistake.

Write down your own if it's not listed

_____
_____
_____
_____
_____
_____
_____
_____

# FRIENDSHIP

## *More on* Chaverut

- **Treasure of Friendships:** *Chaverut*, the Jewish value of friendship, is akin to having a treasure chest filled with valuable gems – our friends. Friends are like precious jewels, each one unique and special, adding sparkle and joy to our lives.

- **Shared Adventures:** Just as a treasure hunt is more exciting with friends by your side, life's adventures become more meaningful when shared with others. *Chaverut* encourages us to build strong, supportive connections with those around us.

- **Being a True Gem:** In *Chaverut*, we learn that being a good friend is like being a shining gem. It involves qualities like kindness, understanding, and being there for one another. True friendship is a treasure that enriches our lives.

- **Navigating Stormy Seas:** Friends are like anchors during stormy times, keeping us grounded and supported. *Chaverut* teaches us the importance of standing by our friends, just as we hope they stand by us when challenges arise.

### And in this superhero journey,

*Chaverut* is like having a treasure chest of friendships - a collection of priceless gems that brighten our days and accompany us on life's incredible journey.
How wonderful is that?

# Heroes Among Us — *Think*

Heroes come in all shapes and sizes. They inspire us, showing that even in challenging times, one person can make a difference. Let's learn from some incredible heroes whose actions embody Jewish values.

## Ruth

Ruth, an inspiring figure from the Bible, embodies the essence of *Chaverut* – the Jewish value of friendship. Her story, found in the Book of Ruth, beautifully illustrates the treasure of friendships and the enduring qualities of a true friend.

**Ruth & Naomi**

In a time long ago, there lived a woman named Ruth. Ruth wasn't originally from the same land as her friend Naomi; they came from different backgrounds. Yet, their friendship was extraordinary.

When difficult times struck, Naomi decided to return to her homeland. Surprisingly, Ruth chose to go with her, uttering these powerful words:

**"Where you go, I will go, and where you stay, I will stay. Your people will be my people, and your God my God."** -Ruth 1:16

Ruth's Wise Choice; illustration from a Bible card 1907

This statement marked the essence of true friendship, transcending differences and embracing a shared journey. Ruth, not originally Jewish, expressed a deep commitment to Naomi and her people, choosing to follow a different path than her own.

As fate unfolded, Ruth's loyalty and kindness didn't go unnoticed. She encountered a man named Boaz, who admired her virtuous character. Eventually, Ruth became part of a lineage that would lead to the birth of King David, a significant figure in Jewish history.

Ruth's story teaches us that genuine friendship knows no boundaries, and sometimes, unexpected connections lead to remarkable outcomes.

Her legacy, as the great-grandmother of King David, highlights the profound impact that acts of kindness and loyalty can have on the course of history.

# Say ♥ BEcome a Hero

Remember, Heroes come in all shapes and sizes. They inspire us, showing that even in challenging times, one person can make a difference.

### You have the power to be a hero in your own life!

**Ruth was a remarkable woman** whose story embodies the essence of *Chaverut*, the Jewish value of friendship.

1. Reflect on a time when you made a commitment to a friend. How did your commitment impact the friendship?

_____
_____

2. Consider a challenging situation a friend went through. How did you demonstrate loyalty and support during that time?

_____
_____

3. Reflect on a friendship where actions spoke louder than words. How did deeds strengthen the bond between you and your friend?

_____
_____

**4. Think about a friend with whom you share differences. How have you embraced those differences to build a stronger friendship?**

_____
_____
_____
_____

**5. How can the story of Ruth inspire you to be a better friend? What qualities from her story resonate with your understanding of true friendship?**

_____
_____
_____
_____

**6. Consider the idea of long-lasting friendships. What actions can you take to ensure that your friendships, like Ruth and Naomi's, stand the test of time and challenges?**

_____
_____
_____
_____

**You have the power to be a hero in your own life!**

# BEcome a Hero To-Do-List

Guess what, heroes don't keep the lessons to themselves; they share it with the world.

## Teach & Inspire Others — Chaverut

**Choose one or more actions to inspire others and spread the lessons of FRIENDSHIP**

**Compliment Chain:**
- Start a chain of compliments among friends.
- Example: Compliment a friend, and encourage them to compliment someone else. Watch the chain of positivity grow.

**Random Acts of Kindness:**
- Perform random acts of kindness for your friends.
- Example: Surprise a friend by helping them with something, like organizing their desk or sharing your snacks.

**Listen and Learn:**
- Practice active listening with your friends.
- Example: When a friend is talking, focus on what they're saying without interrupting.
- Show that you value their thoughts and feelings.

**Friendship Bracelet Exchange:**
- Create and exchange friendship bracelets.
- Example: Make bracelets for your friends with personalized colors or symbols.
- Exchange them as a symbol of your friendship.

**Celebration Circle:**
- Gather to celebrate each other's achievements.
- Example: Share a moment from your week that you're proud of, and
- encourage your friends to do the same. Celebrate together!

These activities not only promote friendship but also enhance communication, empathy, and mutual support among friends. Enjoy mastering *Chaverut*!

# Middot & Mitzvot fun quiz!

## Here are five questions with multiple-choice answers:

**Question 1: What does the Jewish value of *Chaverut* emphasize?**

A. Building sandcastles
B. Making true friendships
C. Climbing trees
D. Collecting seashells

**Question 2: How does *Chaverut* compare friends to?**

A. Precious jewels
B. Spinning tops
C. Colorful balloons
D. Glittering rainbows

**Question 3: What lesson does *Chaverut* teach about life's adventures?**

A. They are more exciting alone
B. They should be avoided
C. They are meaningful when shared
D. They are only for brave people

**Question 4: What is the significance of friends during stormy times in *Chaverut*?**

A. They act as anchors
B. They turn into superheroes
C. They disappear
D. They become treasure maps

**Question 5: How can you be a true friend, embodying the essence of *Chaverut*?**

A. By showing kindness and understanding.
B. By being there for your friends during challenges.
C. By sharing adventures and creating meaningful memories.
D. All of the above.

(Answers on p. 151)

# Chapter Seven

Tikkun Olam
(Repairing the world)

# REPAIRING THE WORLD

## Tikkun Olam

Just as a handyman is adept at fixing things, maintaining order, and making improvements, individuals participating in *Tikkun Olam* act as "Handy people."

Imagine having tools like a wrench, hammer, and screwdriver in your *Tikkun Olam* toolbox. These tools symbolize the actions we take to repair and improve the world around us. We become superheroes of repair.

"Handy people" skillfully work towards creating positive change, addressing issues, and contributing to the betterment of society and the environment.

Using a toolbox of compassion and action, their distinctive powers enable them to repair, heal, and spark positive change in the world around us.

How incredible is that?

"Repairing the world is not a task for you to complete alone, but neither are you free to desist from it."

— Rabbi Tarfon, Pirkei Avot

# How are You feeling today?

Date: _____

# My Mitzvot & Middot Weekly Journal

Describe your mood at this moment with a word/emoji.  Circle the word that fits best.

_____  Happy  Loving  Curious  Grateful  Surprised  Sad  Inspired  Nervous  Bored

## Mitzvot Tracker

**Which mitzvot did you perform this week? Check off the Mitzvot and/or write your own.**

- [ ] Donated to charity.
- [ ] Helped a neighbor.
- [ ] Prayed at the synagogue.
- [ ] Volunteered at a community event.
- [ ] Respected others.
- [ ] Visited someone who is sick.
- [ ] Followed Shabbat rituals.
- [ ] Shared food with someone in need.
- [ ] Fed and played with my pet
- [ ] Studied Jewish text.

## Middot Tracker

**Reflect on your interactions with others**

**Check off the Middot you've practiced this week**

- [ ] **Kindness:** Helped a friend.
- [ ] **Honesty:** Admitted a mistake.
- [ ] **Patience:** Waited for a turn without getting upset.
- [ ] **Respect:** Listened attentively to others.
- [ ] **Compassion:** Comforted a friend in need.
- [ ] **Responsibility:** Completed chores without being asked.
- [ ] **Gratitude:** Thanked someone for their help.
- [ ] **Humility:** Accepted constructive criticism gracefully.
- [ ] **Courage:** Spoke up against unfairness.
- [ ] **Forgiveness:** Pardoned someone for a mistake.

**Write down your own if it's not listed**

**REPAIRING THE WORLD**

# More on Tikkun Olam

- **Building Bridges:** Embracing *Tikkun Olam* turns us into bridge builders. Our tools are like planks that help us construct bridges between people, fostering unity and understanding. We become architects of connection.

- **Kindness Nails:** *Tikkun Olam* includes kindness as a powerful nail in our toolbox. Acts of kindness are the nails that hold together the repairs we make in the world. We become superheroes who hammer kindness into every repair.

- **Compass of Compassion:** *Tikkun Olam* is our compass of compassion. It guides us toward areas that need repair, helping us navigate the path to making a positive impact. We become superheroes who follow the compass of kindness.

- **Gardening Gloves of Growth:** As superheroes of *Tikkun Olam*, we wear gardening gloves. Our hands, armed with kindness, plant seeds of positive change and nurture growth. We become gardeners of a better world.

### And in this superhero journey,

*Tikkun Olam* transforms us into superheroes of repair. It's like having a toolbox that symbolizes our commitment to fixing what's broken and making the world a more compassionate and just place. Our superhero toolbox inspires others to join in the repair work, creating a world where kindness and goodness prevail.

# Heroes Among Us *Think*

Heroes come in all shapes and sizes. They inspire us, showing that even in challenging times, one person can make a difference. Let's learn from some incredible heroes whose actions embody Jewish values.

==Theodore Herzl== was a super visionary guy who lived a while back, (late 1800s.) Now, he wasn't a superhero in a cape, but he did something amazing for the Jewish people.

- **Big Dreamer:** Theodore Herzl had this giant dream - he wanted to find a safe and happy place for Jewish people to live together. It's like he had this massive puzzle, and he worked really hard to figure out how all the pieces fit together.

- **Book Worm:** Herzl loved reading books and thinking about big ideas. He wrote down all his thoughts in a special book, and that book became like a guide for his dream. It's kind of like when you write down your big plans or cool ideas in your notebook!

- **Jewish Hero:** Herzl is often called the father of modern political Zionism. That's a fancy way of saying he played a key role in making the dream of having a Jewish homeland come true.

So, Theodore Herzl wasn't a hero who wore a cape, but he was a hero in a suit with a vision for a brighter future for all Jewish people. Cool, right?

**The Jewish value that would fit Theodore Herzl is *Tikkun Olam* (Repairing the world)**

Theodore Herzl was like a superhero with a big dream! You know how some superheroes want to make the world a better place? Well, Herzl's special power was having a vision for the Jewish people.

Imagine a time when Jewish people didn't have a country to call their own. Herzl looked at the world and thought, "What if we had our very own place?" It's like when you dream of having your own treehouse, but Herzl dreamt of a whole country!

He believed that by having a homeland, Jewish people could be safe and free. So, he started talking to lots of people, sharing his dream, and guess what? Over time, his dream came true, and Israel was born! Herzl's big idea was like a big hug for the Jewish people, giving them a place to call home.

So, when we talk about *Tikkun Olam*, fixing the world, Herzl's dream was his way of making the world a better place for his fellow Jewish friends. Super cool, right?

# Say ♥ BEcome a Hero

Remember, Heroes come in all shapes and sizes. They inspire us, showing that even in challenging times, one person can make a difference.

## You have the power to be a hero in your own life!

**Exploring *Tikkun Olam*: Repairing the World**

Herzl's Vision: "Imagine a world where everyone had a place to call home." Theodore Herzl, like a superhero, dreamed of creating a homeland for the Jewish people.

**1. Can you think of a dream you have that could make the world better?**

_____

_____

**2. Herzl believed in his dream and worked hard to make it a reality. Have you ever worked towards making something you believe in come true? How did it feel when you saw it happen?**

_____

_____

_____

**3. Herzl's dream was like a big hug for the Jewish people, providing them with a safe and free homeland. What kind of things make you feel safe and free, like you're in your own special place?**

_____

_____

**4.** *Tikkun Olam* **means fixing the world. How do you think Herzl's dream of creating Israel is a way of fixing the world for the Jewish people?
Can you think of other ways people can fix the world?**

_____

_____

_____

_____

**5. Just like Herzl had a big dream, what's something small you can do to make the world a better place for someone else? It could be like a little superhero act of kindness!**

_____

_____

_____

_____

**6. If you could dream of making the world a better place, what would your dream be? How could you work towards making that dream come true, even in a small way?**

_____

_____

_____

_____

**You have the power to be a hero in your own life!**

Guess what, heroes don't keep the lessons to themselves; they share it with the world.

## Teach & Inspire Others *Tikkun olam*

**Choose one or more actions to inspire others, spread the lessons of REPAIRING THE WORLD**

**Community Clean-Up Crew:**
- Organize a group to clean up a local park or neighborhood.
- Example: Spend a Saturday morning picking up litter, planting flowers, and making the community more beautiful.

**Tzedakah Treasure Box:**
- Create a Tzedakah (charity) treasure box with your friends.
- Example: Each person contributes spare change to the box.
- When it's full, decide together on a cause to donate the money.

**Eco-Friendly Campaign:**
- Start a campaign to promote eco-friendly practices at school.
- Example: Encourage classmates to use reusable water bottles, reduce paper waste, and recycle. Make posters to raise awareness.

**Caring Card Team:**
- Make and distribute uplifting cards to local Jewish nursing homes or hospitals.
- Example: Create colorful cards with positive messages to brighten the day of residents or patients. Share the joy of giving.

**Planting for Tomorrow:**
- Initiate a tree-planting project in your community.
- Example: Work with local authorities to plant trees in public spaces. It's a sustainable way to contribute to the environment.

These activities help instill the value of *Tikkun Olam*, teaching others that even small actions can contribute to making the world a better place. Enjoy making a positive impact!

# Middot & Mitzvot fun quiz!

**Here are five questions with multiple-choice answers:**

**Question 1: What does the term *Tikkun Olam* mean?**

A. Eating delicious food
B. Fixing the world
C. Playing video games all day
D. Sleeping under the stars

**Question 2: Who is compared to a superhero with a big dream in the context of *Tikkun Olam*?**

A. Moses
B. Theodore Herzl
C. King Solomon
D. Anne Frank

**Question 3: How did Herzl work towards achieving his dream of a homeland for the Jewish people?**

A. By playing music
B. By talking to people and sharing his dream
C. By hiding in a cave
D. By becoming a chef

**Question 4: What is *Tikkun Olam* in action, according to the provided text?**

A. Fixing a broken toy
B. Creating art
C. Fixing the world
D. Reading a book

**Question 5: How does the text suggest kids can contribute to *Tikkun Olam* in their own way?**

A. By eating candy
B. By playing video games
C. By doing small acts of kindness
D. By sleeping all day

(Answers on p. 151)

# Chapter Eight

Pikuach Nefesh
(Saving a life)

# SAVING A LIFE

## Pikuach Nefesh

Did you know that in Judaism, saving a life, *Pikuach Nefesh*, is one of the most valuable and sacred values?

It's the cornerstone of our faith and a guiding principle that teaches us the immense worth of every human life.

*Pikuach Nefesh* is a reminder that we all have the power to be life-savers, promoting a world where the safety and well-being of every person come first.

How incredible is that?

# How are You feeling today?

Date: _____

# My Mitzvot & Middot Weekly Journal

Describe your mood at this moment with a word/emoji. Circle the word that fits best.

Happy   Loving   Curious   Grateful   Surprised   Sad   Inspired   Nervous   Bored

## Mitzvot Tracker

Which mitzvot did you perform this week? Check off the Mitzvot and/or write your own.

- [ ] Donated to charity.
- [ ] Helped a neighbor.
- [ ] Prayed at the synagogue.
- [ ] Volunteered at a community event.
- [ ] Respected others.
- [ ] Visited someone who is sick.
- [ ] Followed Shabbat rituals.
- [ ] Shared food with someone in need.
- [ ] Fed and played with my pet
- [ ] Studied Jewish text.

## Middot Tracker

Reflect on your interactions with others

**Check off the Middot you've practiced this week**

- [ ] **Kindness:** Helped a friend.
- [ ] **Honesty:** Admitted a mistake.
- [ ] **Patience:** Waited for a turn without getting upset.
- [ ] **Respect:** Listened attentively to others.
- [ ] **Compassion:** Comforted a friend in need.
- [ ] **Responsibility:** Completed chores without being asked.
- [ ] **Gratitude:** Thanked someone for their help.
- [ ] **Humility:** Accepted constructive criticism gracefully.
- [ ] **Courage:** Spoke up against unfairness.
- [ ] **Forgiveness:** Pardoned someone for a mistake.

Write down your own if it's not listed

# SAVING A LIFE

## More on Pikuach Nefesh

- **Every Life is Precious:** In the world of *Pikuach Nefesh*, every life is incredibly precious. It doesn't matter who they are, where they come from, or what they believe – the focus is on preserving and safeguarding life above all else.

- **Be a Life-Saver:** *Pikuach Nefesh* inspires us to be like doctors, real-life superheroes ready to jump in and help whenever someone's life is in danger. Whether it's through medical assistance, support, or simply being there for someone, we can all play a role in saving lives.

- **Prioritizing Compassion:** This value teaches us that compassion and empathy are our superpowers. By prioritizing the well-being of others, we become heroes in our own right, contributing to a world where every individual feels valued and protected.

### And in this superhero journey,

> *Pikuach Nefesh* is a reminder that we all have the power to be life-savers, promoting a world where the safety and well-being of every person come first. How incredible is that?

# Heroes Among Us

Heroes come in all shapes and sizes. They inspire us, showing that even in challenging times, one person can make a difference. Let's learn from some incredible heroes whose actions embody Jewish values.

## Henrietta Szold:

Meet Henrietta Szold, a Jewish American leader who lived in the 1800s, and was like a pioneer for healthcare and education. Henrietta founded Hadassah, an organization that went beyond saving lives. Through the establishment of medical services and educational institutions, Szold's work not only saved individual lives but also contributed to the well-being of entire communities.

Henrietta Szold at her home in Jerusalem, 1922

Her dedication helped people recover from illnesses and provided essential knowledge. In essence, Henrietta Szold's impact extended beyond saving lives, making entire communities healthier and happier.

## Queen Esther

Queen Esther, a central figure in the biblical Book of Esther, is renowned for her courage and strategic wisdom. Born as Hadassah, she became the queen of Persia after winning a beauty contest. Esther's heroism unfolded when she learned of a plot to annihilate the Jewish people. Risking her own life, she approached King Ahasuerus, to thwart the plan, revealing her Jewish identity. Esther's bravery and devotion to her people are celebrated during the festival of Purim, emphasizing the significance of courage and faith in the face of adversity.

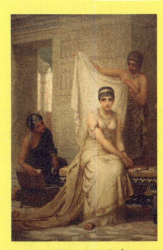
Queen Esther, by Edwin Long, 1878

*Pikuach Nefesh* literally translated as "saving a soul," means that saving a life is the top priority-even more crucial than almost anything else we do. In Jewish tradition, the Talmudic teaching states, **"One who saves a single life is considered as if they saved an entire world."** This principle teaches us that nothing matters more than looking out for each other and making sure everyone is safe and well.

These heroes, though from different times, all believed that saving one life is like saving the whole world, a principle deeply cherished in Jewish values. Whether it's building hospitals like Henrietta or showing courage like Queen Esther, their stories show how important it is to value and protect life in the Jewish tradition.

# Say BEcome a Hero

Remember, Heroes come in all shapes and sizes. They inspire us, showing that even in challenging times, one person can make a difference.

## You have the power to be a hero in your own life!

**Exploring *Pikuach Nefesh*: saving life**

1. **Can you think of everyday situations where safety should be the top priority? How does this connect to the concept of *Pikuach Nefesh*?**

_____

_____

2. **Consider everyday heroes around you who prioritize the safety of others. It could be a lifeguard, a crossing guard, or even a friend who looks out for others. How do these everyday heroes embody the value of *Pikuach Nefesh*?**

_____

_____

3. **Think about Henrietta Szold or Queen Esther. What do you know about their stories, and how do you think their actions reflect the principle of saving one life being like saving the whole world?**

_____

_____

**4. Imagine being in a situation where you have to choose between ensuring someone's safety and completing a personal goal. How would you balance these priorities, keeping *Pikuach Nefesh* in mind?**

___

___

___

___

**5. Reflect on stories you've heard or read about people who risked their own safety to save others. How did their actions impact individuals and communities? How does this align with the idea of saving one life being like saving the whole world?**

___

___

___

___

**6. Think about a time when you or someone you know faced a challenging situation related to health or safety. How did people around you react, and what did you learn from that experience?**

___

___

___

___

**You have the power to be a hero in your own life!**

# BEcome a Hero — To-Do-List

Guess what, heroes don't keep the lessons to themselves; they share it with the world.

## Teach & Inspire Others — Pikuach Nefesh

**Choose one or more actions to inspire others and spread the lessons of SAVING A LIFE**

**Emergency Response Training:**
- Learn how to call 911 and provide necessary information in case of emergencies.
- <u>Example:</u> Practice calling 911 with a parent or guardian. Know your address and be ready to explain the situation.

**Safety Buddy System:**
- Establish a safety buddy system with friends to ensure everyone's well-being.
- <u>Example:</u> Choose a buddy during outdoor activities or outings. Look out for each other and report any potential dangers.

**Emergency Contact List:**
- Create a list of important emergency contacts for quick reference.
- <u>Example:</u> Make a list of phone numbers for parents, guardians, and school staff. Keep it in your backpack for easy access.

**First Aid Basics:**
- Learn basic first aid skills to assist in minor injuries.
- Example: Attend a first aid workshop or watch videos to understand bandaging and emergency procedures. Practice with your family.

**Safety Awareness Posters:**
- Raise awareness about safety by creating informative posters.
- <u>Example:</u> Design posters promoting safety measures like looking both ways before crossing the street. Display them in common areas at school.

By incorporating these actions into your routine, you're actively contributing to a safer environment and mastering the principle of *Pikuach Nefesh*.

# Middot & Mitzvot fun quiz!

### Here are five questions with multiple-choice answers:

**Question 1: What does the term *Pikuach Nefesh* mean in Judaism?**

A. Lighting candles
B. Saving a life
C. Fasting on Yom Kippur
D. Planting trees

**Question 2: According to Jewish teachings, what takes precedence over almost all other religious obligations?**

A. Charity
B. Prayer
C. Preserving life (*Pikuach Nefesh*)
D. Celebrating festivals

**Question 3: In Judaism, what is the significance of the principle "saving one life is like saving a whole world"?**

A. It means every life is equally valuable
B. It highlights the importance of family
C. It emphasizes the role of community
D. It refers to environmental conservation

**Question 4: When faced with a situation involving potential danger to life, what does Jewish law prioritize?**

A. Following traditions
B. Eating candy
C. Preserving life (*Pikuach Nefesh*)
D. Reading a book

**Question 5: In the context of *Pikuach Nefesh*, what is the guiding principle?**

A. Saving a life is a duty
B. Life is sacred, and every moment matters
C. Healthy living is the key to happiness
D. Life-saving actions require community approval

(Answers on p. 151)

# Chapter Nine

Shmirat Halashon
(Being careful about how we speak)

**BEING CAREFUL ABOUT HOW WE SPEAK**

## Shmirat Halashon

Did you know that *Shmirat Halashon*,
the Jewish value of guarding one's speech,
functions as a powerful water filter for our words?

Similar to a water filter that purifies water,
it sifts through our thoughts and expressions,
ensuring only pure and positive words flow through.

reminding us to speak kindly and avoid causing harm.

How refreshing is that?

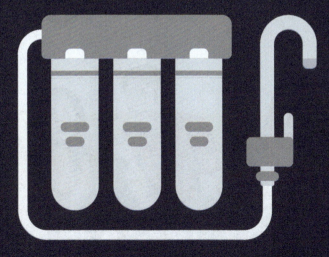

# How are You feeling today?

Date: _____

# My Mitzvot & Middot Weekly Journal

Describe your mood at this moment with a word/emoji. Circle the word that fits best.

_____   Happy   Loving   Curious   Grateful   Surprised   Sad   Inspired   Nervous   Bored

## Mitzvot Tracker

Which mitzvot did you perform this week? Check off the Mitzvot and/or write your own.

- ☐ Donated to charity.
- ☐ Helped a neighbor.
- ☐ Prayed at the synagogue.
- ☐ Volunteered at a community event.
- ☐ Respected others.
- ☐ Visited someone who is sick.
- ☐ Followed Shabbat rituals.
- ☐ Shared food with someone in need.
- ☐ Fed and played with my pet
- ☐ Studied Jewish text.

## Middot Tracker

Reflect on your interactions with others

**Check off the Middot you've practiced this week**

- ☐ **Kindness:** Helped a friend.
- ☐ **Honesty:** Admitted a mistake.
- ☐ **Patience:** Waited for a turn without getting upset.
- ☐ **Respect:** Listened attentively to others.
- ☐ **Compassion:** Comforted a friend in need.
- ☐ **Responsibility:** Completed chores without being asked.
- ☐ **Gratitude:** Thanked someone for their help.
- ☐ **Humility:** Accepted constructive criticism gracefully.
- ☐ **Courage:** Spoke up against unfairness.
- ☐ **Forgiveness:** Pardoned someone for a mistake.

**Write down your own if it's not listed**

# BEING CAREFUL ABOUT HOW WE SPEAK

## *More on* Shmirat Halashon

- **Clarifying Intentions:** In the realm of *Shmirat Halashon*, our speech filter acts like a water purifier, clarifying our intentions. It works to remove impurities, leaving behind words that are clear, genuine, and free from negativity.

- **Words as Crystal Clear Droplets:** This superhero value treats our words as crystal clear droplets. Each word, filtered through the lens of *Shmirat Halashon*, becomes a pure and refreshing contribution to the river of communication, fostering understanding and harmony.

- **Gossip-Repellent Membrane:** *Shmirat Halashon* acts as a gossip-repellent membrane, much like a water filter that removes contaminants. It shields against harmful words, ensuring that our conversations remain free from negativity, rumors, and gossip.

### And in this superhero journey,

> *Shmirat Halashon* encourages us to filter our expressions. Our speech filter becomes a valuable tool in creating a communication environment where words are filtered thoughtfully, fostering positive and uplifting conversations. How refreshing is that?

# Heroes Among Us  *Think*

Heroes come in all shapes and sizes. They inspire us, showing that even in challenging times, one person can make a difference. Let's learn from some incredible heroes whose actions embody Jewish values.

## Chofetz Chaim:

Meet the Chofetz Chaim, a hero of *Shmirat Halashon*! In the late 19th and early 20th centuries, Rabbi Yisrael Meir Kagan, known as the Chofetz Chaim, became a guiding light in promoting the careful use of words.

He was a wise and respected sage, sharing valuable teachings about the destructive nature of *lashon hara*, which means harmful speech.

According to him, *lashon hara* was considered the most harmful of all sins because it had the power to destroy people.

Rabbi Yisrael Meir HaCohen Kagan at prayer

The Chofetz Chaim emphasized the profound impact of our words, stating that:

## "Death and life are in the power of the tongue"

This notion aligns with the biblical wisdom found in Proverbs (18:21):
***"Mavet V'Chayim Beyad HaLashon"***

This means that our speech has the potential to bring both harm and benefit, highlighting the importance of using our words responsibly and promoting positive communication. His teachings serve as a guiding light, encouraging us to be mindful of the power our words hold and to strive for speech that fosters life and positivity.

Born in 1838 in what is now Belarus, the Chofetz Chaim became a revered rabbi and scholar. His legacy includes the compilation of works such as "Chofetz Chaim" and *Shmirat Halashon*, which outline the guidelines for proper speech according to Jewish law.

The Chofetz Chaim's teachings inspire us to be mindful of the words we use, reminding us that our speech has the potential to impact the lives of others significantly. By embracing the principles of *Shmirat Halashon*, we can contribute to a world where communication is thoughtful, positive, and uplifting.

# Say BEcome a Hero

Remember, Heroes come in all shapes and sizes. They inspire us, showing that even in challenging times, one person can make a difference.

## You have the power to be a hero in your own life!

**Exploring *Shmirat Halashon* : guarding one's speech**

1. Reflect on a time when you might have spoken negatively about someone without thinking. How did it make you feel afterward, and what impact do you think it had on the person involved?

___

___

___

2. Consider the phrase "Death and life are in the tongue." How can understanding the power of our words influence the way we communicate with others?

___

___

___

3. Think about a situation where you were a bystander to gossip or negative talk. How did you respond, and what could you do differently in the future to uphold the value of *Shmirat Halashon*?

___

___

# BEcome a Hero — Say

**4.** *Shmirat Halashon* encourages us to filter our speech. What strategies can you develop to pause and think before expressing your thoughts to ensure they are positive and constructive?

_____
_____
_____
_____

**5.** Explore the idea of building a supportive community through *Shmirat Halashon*. How can practicing positive speech contribute to creating a healthier and more uplifting environment?

_____
_____
_____
_____

**6.** Imagine yourself in the shoes of the Chofetz Chaim. If you were a role model for *Shmirat Halashon*, how would you influence those around you to adopt this value in their interactions?

_____
_____
_____
_____

**You have the power to be a hero in your own life!**

Guess what, heroes don't keep the lessons to themselves; they share it with the world.

## Teach & Inspire Others *Shmirat Halashon*

Choose one or more actions to inspire others and spread the lessons of GUARDING ONE'S SPEECH

**Think Before You Speak:**
- Pause and consider your words before speaking to avoid unintentional harm.
- Example: Before sharing a story about someone, ask yourself if it might hurt their feelings or be harmful.

**Kind Words Challenge:**
- Challenge yourself to use only kind and positive words throughout the day.
- Example: Compliment a classmate or friend genuinely. Focus on uplifting language.

**Pause for Empathy:**
- When discussing others, put yourself in their shoes to understand their perspective.
- Example: If someone made a mistake, think about how you would feel if others were discussing your errors.

**Avoid Gossip:**
- Refuse to participate in gossip or negative conversations about others.
- Example: If someone starts gossiping, politely change the topic or walk away. Focus on positive discussions.

**Encourage Positive Speech:**
- Encourage friends to use positive language and speak kindly about others.
- Example: Start a "compliment challenge" with friends, where each person has to give a genuine compliment to someone every day.

Let's embark on an exciting journey to become champions of positive speech! Small steps can lead to big changes.

Are you up for the challenge of *Shmirat Halashon*? Let's make our words a force for good!

**Ready, set, go!**

# Middot & Mitzvot fun quiz!

## Here are five questions with multiple-choice answers:

**Question 1: What does *Shmirat Halashon* mean, and how can filtering our speech positively impact our communication with others?**

A. Protecting the tongue; it helps create positive and uplifting conversations.
B. Using secret codes; it keeps our words mysterious.
C. Ignoring others; it avoids unnecessary discussions.
D. Shouting loudly; it ensures everyone hears our opinions.

**Question 2: How can *Shmirat Halashon* contribute to building a healthy and supportive community?**

A. By spreading gossip; it keeps people informed.
B. By filtering our speech; it fosters positive communication.
C. By criticizing others; it helps them improve.
D. By remaining silent; it avoids unnecessary conflicts.

**Question 3: Why did the Chofetz Chaim consider *lashon hara* (evil speech) as the most destructive of all sins?**

A. Because it's entertaining.
B. Because it builds strong relationships.
C. Because it literally destroys people.
D. Because it promotes honesty.

**Question 4: How can we be like the Chofetz Chaim in our everyday conversations?**

A. By gossiping about others.
B. By sharing secrets.
C. By thinking before we speak and avoiding harmful speech.
D. By criticizing others openly.

**Question 5: What is the significance of the phrase "Death and life are in the tongue" in the context of *Shmirat Halashon*?**

A. It means we should speak loudly.
B. It emphasizes the power of our words to harm or heal.
C. It suggests that silence is the best option.
D. It refers to a magical spell.

(Answers on p. 151)

# Chapter Ten

Tzedakah (Charity)

# CHARITY

## TZEDAKAH

*Tzedakah*, the Jewish value of any act of righteousness like giving to charity, is like a lantern that guides us through the darkness of others' needs.

Each act of generosity is a ray of light that brightens someone's journey, making the world a little warmer and kinder.

# How are You feeling today?

Date: _____

# My Mitzvot & Middot Weekly Journal

Describe your mood at this moment with a word/emoji.  Circle the word that fits best.

| _____ | Happy | Loving | Curious | Grateful | Surprised | Sad | Inspired | Nervous | Bored |

## Mitzvot Tracker

Which mitzvot did you perform this week? Check off the Mitzvot and/or write your own.

- ☐ Donated to charity.
- ☐ Helped a neighbor.
- ☐ Prayed at the synagogue.
- ☐ Volunteered at a community event.
- ☐ Respected others.
- ☐ Visited someone who is sick.
- ☐ Followed Shabbat rituals.
- ☐ Shared food with someone in need.
- ☐ Fed and played with my pet
- ☐ Studied Jewish text.

## Middot Tracker

**Reflect on your interactions with others**

**Check off the Middot you've practiced this week**

- ☐ **Kindness:** Helped a friend.
- ☐ **Honesty:** Admitted a mistake.
- ☐ **Patience:** Waited for a turn without getting upset.
- ☐ **Respect:** Listened attentively to others.
- ☐ **Compassion:** Comforted a friend in need.
- ☐ **Responsibility:** Completed chores without being asked.
- ☐ **Gratitude:** Thanked someone for their help.
- ☐ **Humility:** Accepted constructive criticism gracefully.
- ☐ **Courage:** Spoke up against unfairness.
- ☐ **Forgiveness:** Pardoned someone for a mistake.

Write down your own if it's not listed

# CHARITY

## *More on* Tzedakah

- **Lantern Bearers:** When we practice *Tzedakah*, we become bearers of the lantern of kindness. Our giving is like holding up the lantern to light the way for those in need, helping them find hope and comfort. It's like having a secret mission to bring light to the shadows.

- **Radiating Warmth:** In the world of *Tzedakah*, giving is the flame that radiates warmth. Whether it's a small gesture or a significant contribution, every act of giving adds fuel to the lantern, creating a comforting glow that dispels the darkness.

- **Anonymous Illumination:** *Tzedakah* superheroes often shine their lanterns anonymously, much like a beacon that silently lights up the night. It's not about seeking recognition but about casting a light that makes a difference, even when no one knows it was you.

### And in this superhero journey,

By practicing *Tzedakah*, we become contributors to an illuminated world of kindness. It's like being part of a mission to light up the lives of others, creating a path of compassion and brightness that transforms the darkness into a realm of shared humanity. How brilliantly enlightening is that?

# Heroes Among Us *Think*

Heroes come in all shapes and sizes. They inspire us, showing that even in challenging times, one person can make a difference. Let's learn from some incredible heroes whose actions embody Jewish values.

## Maimonides (Rambam):

Meet A medieval Jewish philosopher and physician, Maimonides is renowned for his teachings on *Tzedakah*. His **Eight Levels of Charity** provide guidance on the different ways one can give, emphasizing the importance of preserving the dignity of those in need.

Maimonides believed that when we want to support someone, it's not just about giving things; it's about helping them learn how to take care of themselves. This teaching resonates with the well-known proverb: **"Give a man a fish, and you feed him for a day; teach a man to fish, and you feed him for a lifetime."** It's like giving them the tools to be strong and independent.

**Moses Maimonides, portrait**

## "Eight Levels of Charity" by Maimonides:

1. **Giving anonymously to an unknown recipient:** The highest form of charity is to give without the recipient knowing who the donor is. This eliminates any sense of shame or embarrassment for the person receiving the assistance.
2. **Giving anonymously to a known recipient:** While still maintaining anonymity, this level involves giving to someone you know. The act preserves the recipient's dignity, as they don't feel beholden to a specific individual.
3. **Giving when the donor is unknown to the recipient:** In this case, the recipient is aware of the donor's identity, but the donor remains unaware of the recipient. This helps prevent any potential embarrassment on the part of the recipient.
4. **Giving directly to the recipient when the donor is known:** Giving openly to someone in need is considered a virtuous act, even if the recipient knows who the donor is. This level encourages community involvement and sets an example for others.
5. **Giving before being asked:** Anticipating the needs of others and offering assistance before they have to ask is a higher form of charity. It shows sensitivity and awareness of the struggles faced by others.
6. **Giving after being asked:** While giving when requested is still a valuable act, it is considered a lesser form of charity compared to providing assistance proactively.
7. **Giving inadequately, but with a smile:** Even if the amount given is not sufficient to fully address the recipient's needs, doing so with kindness and a warm demeanor adds value to the act of charity.
8. **Giving grudgingly:** The lowest level of charity is giving reluctantly or with a sense of resentment. While the act itself may still benefit the recipient, the lack of generosity in spirit diminishes the overall value of the charity.

# Say BEcome a Hero

Remember, Heroes come in all shapes and sizes. They inspire us, showing that even in challenging times, one person can make a difference.

## You have the power to be a hero in your own life!

**Exploring *Tzedakah* : Helping others in need**

1. Think of a recent situation where you noticed someone needed help. What did you do, and how did it make you feel?

_____
_____
_____

2. When deciding to give *Tzedakah*, how do you choose between different causes or individuals in need?

_____
_____
_____

3. Can you share a personal experience where receiving help or kindness from others made a significant impact on you? How did it feel to be on the receiving end?

_____
_____
_____

**4. Imagine you have the opportunity to organize a charity event at your school. What cause would you support, and how would you inspire your classmates to contribute?**

_____
_____
_____
_____

**5. Reflect on a time when you might have hesitated to give or help someone. What was the reason, and what could encourage you to overcome such hesitations in the future?**

_____
_____
_____
_____

**6. Consider a community project aimed at helping those in need. What role would you like to play in such a project, and what positive changes do you hope it brings?**

_____
_____
_____
_____

**You have the power to be a hero in your own life!**

# BEcome a Hero To-Do-List

Guess what, heroes don't keep the lessons to themselves; they share it with the world.

## Teach & Inspire Others — Tzedakah

**Choose one or more actions to inspire others and spread the lessons of CHARITY**

**Kindness Coins Jar:**
- Create a special jar for "Kindness Coins."
- Each day, perform a small act of kindness.
- Drop a coin in the jar to celebrate your good deeds.

**Charity Day Challenge:**
- Designate a day as "Charity Day."
- Collect spare change and donate it to a cause you care about.
- Share your experience with friends to inspire them.

**Tzedakah Treasure Hunt:**
- Organize a Tzedakah Treasure Hunt with friends.
- Hide small notes suggesting acts of kindness or charity.
- Encourage others to find and complete these missions.

**Random Acts of Giving:**
- Surprise someone with a thoughtful gift or gesture.

It could be sharing snacks, helping a friend, or giving a compliment.
Experience the joy of giving without expecting anything in return.

**Family Charity Project:**
- Collaborate with your family on a charity project.
- Choose a cause together and plan how to contribute.

Whether it's donating clothes or raising funds, teamwork makes a difference.

Let the spirit of Tzedakah guide you on this exciting journey of giving and making the world a better place!

# Middot & Mitzvot fun quiz!

## Here are five questions with multiple-choice answers:

**Question 1: Think of a time when you helped someone. How did it feel, and what impact do you think it had on the person you helped?**

A. Made them happy
B. Made them sad
C. Didn't make a difference
D. Confused them

**Question 2: If you had to explain *Tzedakah* to a friend, how would you describe it in your own words?**

A. Giving money to charity
B. Helping others in need
C. Keeping things for yourself
D. Telling secrets to friends

**Question 3: Consider the saying, "Give a man a fish, and you feed him for a day; teach a man to fish, and you feed him for a lifetime." How does this relate to the idea of *Tzedakah*?**

A. It doesn't relate
B. Giving is more important
C. Teaching is more important
D. Both B and C

**Question 4: Why do you think Maimonides emphasized the importance of helping people become self-sufficient?**

A. Because it's easier
B. To respect their dignity and independence
C. It doesn't matter
D. Just for fun

**Question 5: How can you practice Tzedakah in your everyday life, even if you don't have money to give?**

A. Help a friend with their homework
B. Share your lunch with someone who forgot theirs
C. Ignore others and focus on yourself
D. Both A and B

(Answers on p. 151)

# Chapter Eleven

Hodayah (Gratitude)

# GRATITUDE

## Hodayah

*Hodayah*, the Jewish value of gratitude, is like having a magical gratitude journal that turns ordinary moments into extraordinary ones.

It's about appreciating the good things in our lives and spreading positive vibes wherever we go.

Imagine writing in a journal where each word represents moments of gratitude.

*Hodayah* allows us to use the ink of appreciation to record and reflect on the people, experiences, and challenges that shape our lives.

How wonderfully delightful is that?

# How are You feeling today?

Date: _____

# My Mitzvot & Middot Weekly Journal

Describe your mood at this moment with a word/emoji. Circle the word that fits best.

_____  Happy  Loving  Curious  Grateful  Surprised  Sad  Inspired  Nervous  Bored

## Mitzvot Tracker

Which mitzvot did you perform this week? Check off the Mitzvot and/or write your own.

- [ ] Donated to charity.
- [ ] Helped a neighbor.
- [ ] Prayed at the synagogue.
- [ ] Volunteered at a community event.
- [ ] Respected others.
- [ ] Visited someone who is sick.
- [ ] Followed Shabbat rituals.
- [ ] Shared food with someone in need.
- [ ] Fed and played with my pet.
- [ ] Studied Jewish text.

## Middot Tracker

Reflect on your interactions with others

**Check off the Middot you've practiced this week**

- [ ] **Kindness:** Helped a friend.
- [ ] **Honesty:** Admitted a mistake.
- [ ] **Patience:** Waited for a turn without getting upset.
- [ ] **Respect:** Listened attentively to others.
- [ ] **Compassion:** Comforted a friend in need.
- [ ] **Responsibility:** Completed chores without being asked.
- [ ] **Gratitude:** Thanked someone for their help.
- [ ] **Humility:** Accepted constructive criticism gracefully.
- [ ] **Courage:** Spoke up against unfairness.
- [ ] **Forgiveness:** Pardoned someone for a mistake.

**Write down your own if it's not listed**

# GRATITUDE

## More on Hodayah

- **In Pages of Positivity:** Practicing *Hodayah* is like filling the pages of our gratitude journal with positive affirmations. It's about genuinely feeling grateful and creating a written tapestry of interconnected moments that make life beautiful.

- **Kindness Quill:** When we use our *Hodayah* journal, it's like writing with a quill that spreads seeds of kindness. Gratitude has the power to inspire actions that spread kindness, turning an ordinary day into an extraordinary one. It's the magic of saying, "I appreciate you," and cultivating warmth wherever we go.

And did you know that we can start our day with a gratitude prayer, even before stepping out of bed, called *Modeh Ani*?

"*Modeh ani l'fanecha, melech chai v'kayam, shehechezarta bi nishmati b'chemla, raba emunatecha*" – I thank You, living and enduring King, for You have graciously returned my soul within me. Great is Your faithfulness.

A morning ritual that contributes to the richness of our appreciation for the beauty of life!

### And in this superhero journey,

*Hodayah* gives us a gratitude sanctuary, allowing us to find solace in the simple joys and recognize the goodness around us. It's like having a magical journal that becomes a sanctuary of positivity, turning each day into a delightful adventure of thanks. How enchanting is that?

# Heroes Among Us  *Think*

Heroes come in all shapes and sizes. They inspire us, showing that even in challenging times, one person can make a difference. Let's learn from some incredible heroes whose actions embody Jewish values.

## King David:

King David's life is a testament to the value of *Hodayah*, which means gratitude. Born in Bethlehem, David started as a humble shepherd, tending to sheep in his early years. This simple occupation instilled in him a sense of humility and appreciation for the blessings around him.

David's journey took an unexpected turn when the prophet Samuel anointed him as the future king of Israel. Despite facing challenges and adversaries, David approached each situation with gratitude and a deep faith in God. His music, particularly the Psalms he composed, reflects expressions of thanksgiving and praise. Also, he was King Solomon's father.

King David Playing the Harp (1622) by Gerard van Honthorst

## David & Goliath

**The Star of David**

One notable event in David's life was his confrontation with the giant Goliath. With a sling and stones, David faced this formidable foe, relying on his skills and trust in God. His victory showcased not only bravery but also a grateful acknowledgment of God's guidance.

The *Magen David*, a symbol associated with Judaism, became linked to David's legacy over time, symbolizing unity and the enduring connection between God and the Jewish people. David's life teaches us the importance of expressing gratitude in every circumstance, no matter how humble or grand, and recognizing the source of our blessings.

## The Hebrew Bible & Psalms

The Hebrew Bible, also known as the Tanakh, consists of 24 books that are divided into 3 main sections: The **Torah** (5 books), **Nevi'im** (Prophets / 8 books), and **Ketuvim** (Writings/11 books). The Book of Psalms, containing 150 poems and songs, is part of the third section, *Ketuvim*.

## Helleu-Yah / Psalm 150

As king, David's gratitude extended to the establishment of Jerusalem as the capital and the bringing of the Ark of the Covenant to the city. The Psalms he wrote, including Psalm 150, highlight his thankfulness and devotion to God.

The psalm concludes with the Hebrew word **"Hallelu-Yah,"** which translates to "Praise God" in English. "*Hallelu-Yah*" is an expression of joy, gratitude, and exaltation, capturing the essence of praising God with all one's heart.

# Say ❤️ BEcome a Hero

Remember, Heroes come in all shapes and sizes. They inspire us, showing that even in challenging times, one person can make a difference.

## You have the power to be a hero in your own life!

**Exploring *Hodayah* : Gratitude**

1. Think about something simple, like a beautiful sunrise or a kind gesture from a friend. How does acknowledging and appreciating these small things make you feel?

___

___

___

2. Reflect on a challenging situation you faced recently. Can you find something positive or a lesson learned from that experience that you're grateful for?

___

___

___

3. Consider the people in your life, such as family, friends, or teachers. What are some specific actions they've taken that you're grateful for, and have you expressed your gratitude to them?

___

___

**4. Imagine you woke up tomorrow with only the things you were thankful for today. What would you still have, and how does that perspective change your outlook on your current life?**

_____
_____
_____
_____

**5. Think about a time when you received help from someone. How did their assistance impact you, and what steps can you take to pay that kindness forward?**

_____
_____
_____
_____

**6. Reflect on your achievements, whether big or small. What efforts did you put into reaching those goals, and what support did you receive from others along the way that you're grateful for?**

_____
_____
_____
_____

**You have the power to be a hero in your own life!**

# BEcome a Hero  *To-Do-List*

Guess what, heroes don't keep the lessons to themselves; they share it with the world.

## Teach & Inspire Others  *Hodayah*

**Choose one or more actions to inspire others and spread the lessons of GRATITUDE**

**Gratitude Journal:**
- Begin a Gratitude Journal.
- Each day, write down three things you're thankful for.
- Reflect on the positive aspects of your life.

**Thank You Cards:**
- Design and create Thank You cards.
- Express gratitude to friends, family, or teachers.
- Deliver or mail the cards to make someone's day.
- 

**Compliment Chain:**
- Start a Compliment Chain in your class or among friends.
- Share genuine compliments about each other.
- Create a visual chain to showcase the positivity.

**Gratitude Circle:**
- Form a Gratitude Circle with friends.
- Take turns sharing something you appreciate about each person.
- Foster a culture of gratitude and positivity.

**Acts of Appreciation:**
- Perform small acts of kindness to show appreciation.
- Help a friend with their homework or chores.
- Acknowledge and thank those who contribute to your daily life.

Embrace the power of gratitude and watch how it transforms your perspective and relationships!

# Middot & Mitzvot fun quiz!

## Here are five questions with multiple-choice answers:

**Question 1: What is the central principle of *Hodayah* (Gratitude) in Judaism?**

A. Giving and receiving gifts
B. Focusing on the positive aspects of life and acknowledging them with thanks
C. Celebrating achievements
D. Praying regularly for blessings

**Question 2: How does the concept of *Hodayah* encourage us to view challenges?**

A. Ignore challenges and focus on positive aspects only
B. Complain about challenges to express frustration
C. See challenges as opportunities for growth and learning
D. Avoid challenges at all costs

**Question 3: In what ways can you express *Hodayah* in your daily life?**

A. By only saying thanks when someone does something big for you
B. Ignoring positive aspects of your day
C. Acknowledging and appreciating the small moments and kindness around you
D. Complaining about everything that goes wrong

**Question 4: How does practicing *Hodayah* benefit our relationships with others?**

A. It doesn't affect relationships
B. It can create a positive and grateful atmosphere, strengthening connections
C. It leads to jealousy among friends
D. It makes you appear weak to others

**Question 5: What is the role of *Hodayah* in fostering a sense of responsibility toward those in need?**

A. It has no connection to helping others
B. It encourages indifference toward those in need
C. It inspires us to recognize our blessings and help others in return
D. It promotes selfishness

(Answers on p. 151)

# Chapter Twelve

N'divut (Generosity)

# GENEROSITY

## N'divut

*N'divut*, the Jewish value of generosity, is like being part of a flowing river of opportunities to share and uplift others.

It's about embracing the current of kindness, enriching the lives of those around us as we navigate through the journey of giving.

Imagine having a source that, when tapped into, releases waves of kindness and support.

That's what N'divut does- it connects us to the wellspring of generosity, allowing us to make a positive impact and turning ordinary moments into extraordinary opportunities to spread goodwill.

How incredible is that?

# How are you feeling today?

Date: _____

# My Mitzvot & Middot Weekly Journal

Describe your mood at this moment with a word/emoji. Circle the word that fits best.

| _____ | Happy | Loving | Curious | Grateful | Surprised | Sad | Inspired | Nervous | Bored |

## Mitzvot Tracker

Which mitzvot did you perform this week? Check off the Mitzvot and/or write your own.

- [ ] Donated to charity.
- [ ] Helped a neighbor.
- [ ] Prayed at the synagogue.
- [ ] Volunteered at a community event.
- [ ] Respected others.
- [ ] Visited someone who is sick.
- [ ] Followed Shabbat rituals.
- [ ] Shared food with someone in need.
- [ ] Fed and played with my pet
- [ ] Studied Jewish text.

## Middot Tracker

Reflect on your interactions with others

**Check off the Middot you've practiced this week**

Write down your own if it's not listed

- [ ] **Kindness:** Helped a friend.
- [ ] **Honesty:** Admitted a mistake.
- [ ] **Patience:** Waited for a turn without getting upset.
- [ ] **Respect:** Listened attentively to others.
- [ ] **Compassion:** Comforted a friend in need.
- [ ] **Responsibility:** Completed chores without being asked.
- [ ] **Gratitude:** Thanked someone for their help.
- [ ] **Humility:** Accepted constructive criticism gracefully.
- [ ] **Courage:** Spoke up against unfairness.
- [ ] **Forgiveness:** Pardoned someone for a mistake.

# GENEROSITY

## More on N'divut

- **Generosity Ripples:** Practicing *N'divut* creates ripples of generosity. It's not just about giving material things; it's about sharing joy, compassion, and support. Each act of generosity creates a ripple effect, touching the lives of others and making the world a brighter and more compassionate place.

- **Heartfelt Giving:** When we embrace *N'divut*, it's like discovering a heart of gold within ourselves. Generosity becomes a natural flow from our compassionate hearts, and our actions reflect the kindness and warmth that we carry within.

- **Transformative Giving:** *N'divut* is transformative giving. It goes beyond the ordinary and turns simple acts of kindness into extraordinary gifts. It's the river that turns everyday moments into opportunities to uplift others and contribute to creating a world filled with compassion.

### And in this superhero journey,

> Acts of *N'divut* are intertwined in various Jewish teachings and traditions? From supporting those in need to contributing to charitable causes, our generous actions become currents that flow through the river of kindness, creating a tapestry of goodwill throughout our lives.

 # Heroes Among Us

Heroes come in all shapes and sizes. They inspire us, showing that even in challenging times, one person can make a difference. Let's learn from some incredible heroes whose actions embody Jewish values.

## Moses Montefiore:

Moses Montefiore (1784–1885) was a British Jewish philanthropist and financier known for his exceptional acts of generosity.

Moses Montefiore's journey towards becoming a symbol of *N'divut* (generosity) was shaped by his personal experiences and a deep commitment to making a positive impact on the lives of others. Born in Livorno, Italy, in 1784, Montefiore was of Sephardic Jewish descent.

His family moved to England when he was a child, and he later became a successful financier and banker.

**Sir Moses Montefiore painted in 1881**

Montefiore's financial success provided him with the means to pursue philanthropic endeavors. However, it was his profound sense of compassion and a strong connection to his Jewish heritage that fueled his commitment to acts of generosity. Witnessing the challenges faced by Jewish communities around the world, Montefiore felt a deep responsibility to contribute to their well-being.

**The mill in 1858**

## Montefiore Windmill

One of his most remarkable contributions was the establishment of the Montefiore Windmill in Jerusalem in 1857. This windmill served as a practical solution to the city's grain milling problem, providing a sustainable and efficient source of flour for the local population.

## Yemin Moshe neighborhood

Montefiore's generosity also extended to the development of the Yemin Moshe neighborhood in Jerusalem, named after him. He supported the construction of homes, a hospital, and other facilities, aiming to improve the living conditions of the residents.

**View of Yemin Moshe by Meir Feder 2011**

# Say ♥ BEcome a Hero

Remember, Heroes come in all shapes and sizes. They inspire us, showing that even in challenging times, one person can make a difference.

## You have the power to be a hero in your own life!

**Exploring *N'divut* : Generosity**

1. Reflect on a time when you witnessed an act of generosity. How did it make you feel, and did it inspire you to be more generous in your own actions?

___
___
___

2. Consider the concept of giving more than is necessary or customary. In what ways can you incorporate this idea of going above and beyond into your daily life to cultivate a spirit of generosity?

___
___
___

3. Think about the impact of Moses Montefiore's acts of generosity on the communities he supported. How can your own acts of kindness and giving contribute positively to the well-being of those around you?

___
___
___

**4. Reflect on your own resources, whether time, money, or skills. How can you identify opportunities to share these resources with an open heart, embodying the spirit of *N'divut* in your actions?**

_____
_____
_____
_____

**5. Consider the idea that generosity extends beyond material gifts and can include kindness, empathy, and understanding. How can you incorporate these non-material aspects of generosity into your interactions with others?**

_____
_____
_____
_____

**6. Imagine a scenario where you have the means to make a significant positive impact on a community or cause. What steps can you take to plan and execute a generous act that aligns with your values and beliefs?**

_____
_____
_____
_____

**You have the power to be a hero in your own life!**

# BEcome a Hero To-Do-List

Guess what, heroes don't keep the lessons to themselves; they share it with the world.

## Teach & Inspire Others  N'divut

Choose one or more actions to inspire others and spread the lessons of GENEROSITY

**Kindness Coupons:**
- Create "Kindness Coupons" with acts of generosity.
- Offer them to friends or family members.
- Redeemable for small acts of assistance or support.

**Sharing Circle:**
- Initiate a Sharing Circle with friends.
- Share toys, books, or treats with each other.
- Experience the joy of giving and receiving.

**Volunteer Project:**
- Identify a simple volunteer project in your community.
- Participate in activities that help others.
- Discover the fulfillment that comes from giving your time.

**Generosity Jar:**
- Set up a "Generosity Jar" at home or school.
- Whenever you witness an act of generosity, write it down and place it in the jar.
- Reflect on the positive impact of generosity.

**Random Acts of Kindness:**
- Engage in random acts of kindness.
- Hold the door for someone, share snacks, or offer a kind word.
- Create a ripple effect of generosity in your daily life.

Let the spirit of *N'divut* guide you on this exciting journey of giving and making the world a better place!

# Middot & Mitzvot fun quiz!

**Here are five questions with multiple-choice answers:**

**Question 1: What does the Jewish value of *N'divut* emphasize?**

A. Withholding resources
B. Giving more than is necessary
C. Taking more than is customary
D. Avoiding acts of kindness

**Question 2: Who is mentioned as an example of generosity in the Jewish tradition?**

A. Moses Montefiore
B. King Solomon
C. Queen Esther
D. Ruth

**Question 3: What does the phrase "an outstretched arm" symbolize in the context of generosity?**

A. Withholding help
B. Selfishness
C. Open-handed giving
D. Stinginess

**Question 4: How can generosity be expressed besides giving material gifts?**

A. Withholding empathy
B. Showing kindness and understanding
C. Ignoring others' needs
D. Hoarding resources

**Question 5: In what ways can individuals cultivate a spirit of generosity?**

A. By taking more than is customary
B. By avoiding acts of kindness
C. By giving more than is necessary
D. By being selfish

(Answers on p. 151)

141

#Peace Starts with Values

# We Are Created

B'TZELEM ELOHIM
(IN THE IMAGE OF GOD)

"Imagine all the people living life in peace." – John Lennon

# Key
# Words
# Review

# REVIEW     BOOK ONE: CHAPTERS 1-12

***Hachnasat Orchim* (Hospitality):** Emphasizes the value of welcoming guests, fostering goodwill, inclusion, and openness within communities.

***Shalom* (Peace):** Central to Judaism, Shalom promotes inner and outer peace, emphasizing harmony in relationships and the world.

***Din / Rachamim* (Justice/Mercy):** Balancing justice and mercy, this value encourages fair treatment while recognizing the importance of compassion.

***Teshuvah* (Repentance):** Acknowledging mistakes and seeking repentance contributes to personal growth and reconciliation.

***Emunah* (Faith):** Faith in God and trust in divine guidance play a fundamental role in Jewish spirituality.

***Chaverut* (Friendship):** Values the importance of meaningful connections, promoting supportive and enduring friendships.

***Tikkun Olam* (Repairing the World):** Highlights the responsibility to address global issues and contribute to a more harmonious world.

***Pikuach Nefesh* (Saving a Life):** Prioritizes saving lives, even if it requires breaking ritual laws, emphasizing the sanctity of life.

***Shmirat Halashon* (Guarding One's Speech):** Stresses the importance of using words wisely to prevent harm and promote understanding.

***Tzedakah* (Charity):** Act of giving to those in need builds compassion and equity, forming a foundation for a more peaceful society.

***Hodayah* (Gratitude):** Cultivating gratitude for blessings inspires a desire to help others who are less fortunate.

***N'divut* (Generosity):** Encourages a generous spirit, inspiring people to give of their time and resources with an open heart.

# IN BOOK TWO YOU'LL FIND: CHAPTERS 13-25

**Someich Noflim / Rofei Holim (Lifting up the Fallen/Healing the Sick):** Calls for support and assistance to those in need, contributing to healing and upliftment.

**Gevurah (Heroism):** Heroism is about strength of character, conquering base impulses, and standing up for one's beliefs.

**Ometz Lev (Courage):** Encourages the courage to stand up for what's right and new ideas, contributing to a more peaceful world.

**Tochachah (Rebuke, Speaking Truth to Power):** Promotes speaking up against wrongdoing, fostering accountability and justice.

**Bal Tashchit / Sh'mirat HaTeva (Preserving the Environment):** Emphasizes responsibility for environmental stewardship and conservation.

**Talmud Torah (Study of Jewish Texts):** Sustaining Jewish culture and values through the study of sacred texts.

**Gemilut Hasadim (Acts of Lovingkindness):** Encourages acts of kindness and benevolence, fostering a compassionate and caring society.

**Mechuyavut (Responsibility):** Acknowledges the importance of fulfilling one's responsibilities to oneself, others, and the community.

**Simchah (Joy):** Values finding joy in life's blessings and moments, contributing to overall well-being.

**Yosher / Emet (Integrity/Truth):** Encourages living with integrity by aligning actions with beliefs, fostering honesty and trust.

**Yozmah (Initiative):** Acknowledges the importance of taking initiative and being proactive in personal and communal endeavors.

**Manhigut (Leadership):** Recognizes the significance of effective and ethical leadership in guiding communities and promoting positive change.

**Ahavat Yisrael (Love of Israel):** Encourages love and support for the Jewish people, fostering unity and connection within the community.

# FOCUS
## ON THE GOOD

# Multiple Choice Quiz Answer Key

# Multiple Choice Quiz Answer Key (Book 1 + Book 2)

1. **Hachnasat Orchim** (Hospitality) — 1.B, 2.B, 3.B, 4.B, 5.C
2. **Shalom** (Peace) **Rodef Shalom** (Pursuing Peace) — 1.B, 2.C, 3.B, 4.B, 5.C
3. **Din / Rachamim** (Justice/Mercy) — 1.A, 2.C, 3.B, 4.B, 5.C
4. **Teshuvah** (Repentance) — 1.B, 2.C, 3.C, 4.C, 5.C
5. **Emunah** (Faith) — 1.C, 2.D, 3.D, 4.D, 5.D
6. **Chaverut** (Friendship) — 1.B, 2.A, 3.C, 4.A, 5.D
7. **Tikkun Olam** (Repairing the world) — 1.B, 2.B, 3.B, 4.C, 5.C
8. **Pikuach Nefesh** (Saving a life) — 1.B, 2.C, 3.A, 4.C, 5.B
9. **Shmirat Halashon** (Being careful about how we speak) — 1.A, 2.B, 3.C, 4.C, 5.B
10. **Tzedakah** (Charity) — 1.A, 2.B, 3.D, 4.B, 5.D
11. **Hodayah** (Gratitude) — 1.B, 2.C, 3.C, 4.B, 5.C
12. **N'divut** (Generosity) — 1.B, 2.A, 3.C, 4.B, 5.C
13. **Somech Noflim/Rofei Holim** (Lifting up the fallen/Healing the sick) — 1.B, 2.B, 3.B, 4.C, 5.B
14. **Gevurah** (Heroism) — 1.A, 2.B, 3.B, 4.C, 5.D
15. **Ometz Lev** (Courage) — 1.C, 2.D, 3.B, 4.B, 5.C
16. **Tochachah** (rebuke, speaking truth to power) — 1.B, 2.B, 3.B, 4.C, 5.B
17. **Bal Tashchit/Sh'mirat HaTeva** (Taking care of the environment) — 1.B, 2.B, 3.B, 4.D, 5.B
18. **Talmud Torah** Studying Jewish text — 1.B, 2.B, 3.B, 4.D, 5.B
19. **Gemilut Hasadim** (Acts of lovingkindness) — 1.B, 2.C, 3.B, 4.C, 5.C
20. **Mechuyavut** (Responsibility) — 1.B, 2.B, 3.B, 4.C, 5.C
21. **Simchah** (Joy) — 1.B, 2.C, 3.C, 4.C, 5.C
22. **Yosher/Emet** (Integrity/Truth) — 1.B, 2.C, 3.B, 4.C, 5.B
23. **Yozmah** (Initiative) — 1.B, 2.C, 3.B, 4.B, 5.B
24. **Manhigut** (Leadership) — 1.B, 2.A, 3.C, 4.B, 5.C
25. **Ahavat Yisrael** (Love of Israel) — 1.B, 2.B, 3.B, 4.B, 5.B

# Your words Matter

Hope you're having a blast with Mensch World
**HOW TO BE A JEW TODAY - BECOMING THE BEST YOU!**

Quick peek behind the curtain - Yep, it's me, Rabbi Yakira, a growth writer, who loves creating content that helps you and I become the best version of ourselves. I'm obsessed with personal growth, music, art, self-help, and, like you, daily defeating what I now call The Doubt Dragon 🐉
Oh, and did I mention I'm a proud mother of 3 girls?

Here's my picture, so you know I'm a real person, not just a literary robot!
Based in sunny Los Angeles, CA, and you can find me online at YakiraYedidia.com

Now, onto the good stuff - **your review!**
Your feedback isn't just gold; it's the whole treasure chest!

So, if you've got a sec and a sprinkle of fairy dust to spare, consider leaving a review. Whether it's a quick shout-out or a a detailed critique, it helps shape the future of this adventure.

And guess what? When you drop a review, I'm all ears!
Together, we'll make this book journey even more epic!

Thanks for being part of the adventure!

Catch you on the flip side,

Yakira.

**Amazon review** help us reach more readers. This link will take you directly to Amazon.com review page for this book.
Thank You!

https://hebrewguru.com/amazon-book-review/

# Explore Mensch World Books & Journals!

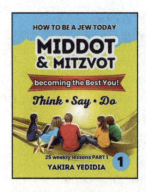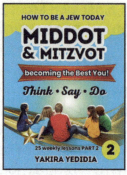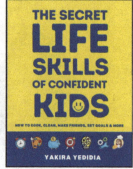
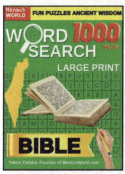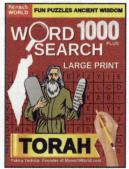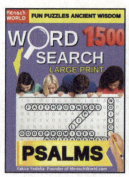
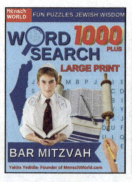

www.MenschWorld.com

Made in the USA
Coppell, TX
09 September 2024

37020338R10090